DIGITAL STORYTELLING

DIGITAL STORYTELLING

The Rise of User-Generated Content

Karam Singh Sethi

NEW DEGREE PRESS

DIGITAL STORYTELLING
The Rise of User-Generated Content

ISBN

978-1-63676-906-6   *Paperback*
978-1-63676-970-7   *Kindle Ebook*
978-1-63730-074-9   *Digital Ebook*

*For Eliza, who has made me more intentional,
patient, and purposeful. I would not have wanted
to spend the pandemic with anyone else.*

I love you.

CONTENTS

———

INTRODUCTION

ANTHONY BOURDAIN'S UNLIKELY IMPACT ON THE WORLD OF STORY

———

I never paid much attention to famous people. Both my brother and sister work in the entertainment industry, so I was desensitized to the world of celebrities from an early age.

But I grieved for Anthony Bourdain when I found out he hanged himself in 2018.

Kitchen Confidential, his inaugural book, was one of the first I can remember reading for pleasure and not at the behest of a teacher or parent.

It had drugs, obscene language, antiheroes, kitchen brawls, and a moody yet earnest narrator—everything a young awkward adolescent boy wanted. But it was also a deeply personal look into Bourdain's emotions as a young man. He connected with readers through a series of personal anecdotes and real-life events—telling us how he *felt* as if he'd never expressed his real emotions before writing them down.

America doesn't socialize young men to talk like that. Reading about a man looking inward was completely foreign to me.

His TV shows were equally intimate. But with faces now appearing on screens instead of on the page, he tried to tell the stories of others. He didn't regularly travel to popular destinations or put out "food porn" that would help drive book sales.

Bourdain evolved from a nonconformist chef/writer into a renowned archetype for the American traveler. Fans from Myanmar to the Ozarks appreciate his satirical yet somehow flattering dialogue that uses food as a lens through which to analyze people and culture.

Shows like *No Reservations* and *Chef's Tour* can be found in some of the most rural areas of the world (as I can personally attest to after finding Bourdain's face blown up on makeshift pop-up screens outside food stalls in Malaysia), demonstrating just how far-reaching his fame is.

He told stories he thought deserved more attention. His shows focused the spotlight on unsung heroes around the world, from activists to street cooks, who, Bourdain believed, didn't get the credit they deserved.

He was on a mission to tell the personal stories behind headline news from the perspective of the people on the ground.

The inaugural episode of his CNN series *Anthony Bourdain: Parts Unknown* is a prime example of this. In it, Bourdain takes on an extraordinary undertaking: explaining the complex multinational country of Myanmar in a short sixty-minute documentary-style video series.

Mired by over fifty years of colonization and civil war, Myanmar's history and sociopolitical dynamics are complicated, to say the least. Bourdain realized he wouldn't be able to do justice to the country's history by taking pretty pictures of food—nor was he a historian or a professor.

But what mattered most were the perspectives of the people. So, in the same style in which he told his own story in *Kitchen Confidential*, he focused on dissecting Myanmar through the eyes of the Burmese.

In the documentary, Bourdain interviewed Zarni Bo, a man who had spent six years of his life in prison. Under the backdrop of a café straight out of a Graham Greene novel, the two discussed Bo's experience in Myanmar. He was an activist and an outspoken critic of the military-run government and was punished for it. After spending his time in prison he was able to see his country open up to the world and slowly enact more equitable policies across its many ethnic groups.

Photograph of a boy walking his bike down an alleyway in Yangon, Myanmar. Shot by me.

Bourdain also interviewed Aung San Suu Kyi, prominent activist turned political leader. The two discussed the human rights leader's upbringing and experiences during her infamous fifteen years under house arrest.

"There's something amazing about meeting people who have been unable to speak. Now, they're able to tell their stories, unguarded," Bourdain said of his experience in Myanmar.[1]

He was able to tell the story of an entire country through its people, and that didn't stop with Myanmar.

He used his unfiltered raw style while shooting the fourteenth episode of season two of *No Reservations* in Lebanon. In July

---

1   "Myanmar," Part's Unknown, Episode 1, Directed by Anthony Bourdain, April 2013.

2006, Bourdain and a four-member crew witnessed the Israeli airstrikes in Beirut while filming. Instead of scrapping the episode and running to safety, they decided to capture the historic moment in which the country slid back into war on camera.

They filmed smoke billowing atop the international airport, interviewed young Beiruties as they partied through the familiar sounds of explosions, and gave an invaluable firsthand account of how expatriates escaped Lebanon during the attack, reporting all through the eyes of people.

Prominent Lebanese journalist, Kim Ghattas, discussed this historic moment in TV and Bourdain's storytelling method in *The Atlantic*.

"Bourdain never made it about Bourdain—Lebanon was the story. And even during the dramatic scene of his departure, on a ship surrounded by Marines and hundreds of other evacuees—Americans and dual citizens—his focus remained on Lebanon and the distraught faces of its people, leaving behind country and family, uncertain of whether they'd ever return," Ghattas writes.[2]

Through the eyes of their people, Bourdain not only helped tell the story of countries like Lebanon and Myanmar but also gave viewers hope for the future of these developing nations.

Bourdain showed me how valuable and powerful a personal narrative approach to storytelling is in getting your message across. If wielded properly, it can be used to increase

2   Kim Ghattas, "How Lebanon Transformed Anthony Bourdain," The Atlantic, June 9, 2018.

donations, shift the tides of an election, stop wars, and transform the world's perspective of a country.

In his display of sincere empathy and cultural exchanges, Bourdain inadvertently made colossal contributions to American diplomacy. He promoted a more endearing side of America—one that's constantly self-critical, contemplative, growing, and learning.

By conveying these personal stories, he created a more sympathetic perspective of outside cultures to Americans (an accomplishment the State Department could only dream of), while also showing the world a more humble and introspective view of the American psyche (contrary to the common trope of loud, braggadocios, and entitled Americans).

In a way, he's done more to spread awareness around international issues than any other politician or publicist. For his work, Bourdain won eight Emmy awards, from categories like Outstanding Writing for a Nonfiction Program in 2016 to Outstanding Informational Series in 2019.

Even after he died in 2018, he was still winning awards. We weren't done acknowledging just how groundbreaking his storytelling work was for the world.

The way Bourdain told stories is more important now than ever before.

With the rise of user-generated content (UGC) and social media, storytelling is the most powerful weapon we have. And it can be used for good—or evil.

That's what this book is about: the distinct rise of UGC, the personal narrative approach to stories, and how the powers that be in politics, business, and culture use content as an instrument to serve their own needs.

We're in uncertain and even dangerous times when it comes to storytelling. As bad actors like President Trump utilize UGC to lie and manipulate, we are realizing just how easy it is to trust a good storyteller.

We're also coming to terms with our overabundance of empathy, which politicians, corporations, and those in leadership positions often exploit.

After nine years of working in marketing, from consulting for the Pentagon to writing for IBM, I've learned a lot. The chase for clicks and money has blurred the line between nonfiction and fiction. I've seen firsthand how the drive for power and influence has corrupted good people into telling lies through stories. And I've also witnessed the power of authentic storytelling to influence positive change.

Storytelling tools have evolved so dramatically over the past two decades that many of us are racing to figure out how and when to tell our stories. The flood of noisy irreverent content on Twitter and Instagram are just a few examples of this.

I wrote this book to explain why we're seeing so many more stories in TV, movies, documentaries, social media, advertisements, and even in the built environment. If we understand the power personal narrative storytelling can have over us, maybe more of us will be cautious and purposeful when telling our own stories.

I also attempt to break down beneficiaries of personal narratives into three segments: *socially conscious storytellers, nefarious storytellers,* and *self-infatuated storytellers.* Socially conscious storytellers can benefit the most from the democratization of storytelling tools as they can use stories to drive social change and often do not have the same access to resources as those in power. Nefarious storytellers aim to use the rise of new media technology to gaslight, manipulate, lie, and corrupt reality. And self-infatuated storytellers are the majority of users on the Internet who use personal narratives to escape reality, pass the time, earn money, or satisfy narcissistic desires. This segment, which includes big tech brands, does not necessarily have altruistic goals, but they don't have ill intent either.

I hope by providing some much-needed context around the current state of digital storytelling, this book will serve as a helpful guide for those entering rapidly changing creative marketing professions like content strategists, brand strategists, designers, writers, or directors. And even if you're not in marketing, I hope this book will give you a glimpse behind the curtain of how stories are told. Hopefully it will help you feel like a more informed consumer of content, as the information we consume from brands, politicians, and news media increasingly influences so much of our own thinking and decision making.

In this book, we'll go back in time and look at the Bible, one of the first and most widely known uses of story as a tool to influence. Then, I'll fast forward to movies like *Star Wars* and *Indiana Jones* and analyze our recent obsession with the story of brands like Google and Facebook. And, of course, I'll take a look into the new rise of the reality TV celebrities.

By providing present and historical context, I will create awareness around the tool of UGC. And, hopefully, I will show you how to use it ethically and authentically.

CHAPTER 1

STORYTELLING THROUGH THE AGES

Human interest stories—they cloud the
issues and fog the mind.

KENT BROCKMAN, THE SIMPSONS

Stories are powerful. Leaders across generations, cultures, businesses, and politics have always known this. As I'm writing this against the backdrop of the 2020 presidential election between Joe Biden and Donald Trump, two well-trained storytellers, I recall a story about Abraham Lincoln I heard in graduate school.

During the Illinois Republican Convention of 1860, two men walked on stage in front of a crowd of 3,000 people in a makeshift 900-seat hall. One was Abraham Lincoln's second cousin, John Hanks, and the other was Hanks's good friend, Isaac D. Jennings.[3]

---

3   "Railsplitter," House Divided, published September 24, 2010.

Immediately following Lincoln's nomination for president, they marched on stage holding two fence rails and a placard. The placard read:

"Abraham Lincoln, the Rail Candidate for President in 1860. Two rails from a lot of 3,000 made in 1830 by Thos. Hanks and Abe Lincoln—whose father was the first pioneer of Macon County."[4]

The sign painter was wrong about Hanks's first name and also incorrect about Thomas Lincoln's (father of Abraham Lincoln) status as an early settler in Illinois.

The crowd responded with such loud applause that part of the ceiling collapsed.

The stunt was well timed. Hanks and Jennings declared the nickname after Lincoln was nominated but before voting had begun. As the story of the incident spread across voting white males in the following days, Lincoln officially picked up the tag "The Rail Splitter Candidate." The name helped him win over enough delegate votes to become the official nominee of the Illinois Republican Party.

Lincoln was never a professional rail splitter; he was first and foremost a prominent lawyer. But that didn't matter to people.

Jennings and Hanks's support was not simply a sincere celebration of Lincoln but a well-orchestrated stunt, masterminded by Richard Oglesby, a supporter of Lincoln. Why

---

4   Martin Tullai, "Abe Lincoln, Rail Splitter," The Baltimore Sun, February 13, 1995.

did Oglesby want to highlight a seemingly inconsequential aspect of Lincoln's story? The answer lies within the makeup of white male voters in the late nineteenth century (essentially all voters at the time).

For all intents and purposes, Lincoln was an elite and a dreamer. He was well educated and spoke in complex prose. Though he was beloved, questions remained among delegates about his electability across socioeconomic lines. He was far from a man of the people.

Oglesby wanted to fix that.

He knew he needed to make Lincoln appear more humble and working class to become electable. Lincoln needed to appeal not just to lawyers but to axe men, butchers, blacksmiths, fishermen, bricklayers, and carpenters to secure the nomination. When Oglesby found out about Lincoln's ability to split rail adequately, he traveled to find wood Lincoln *may* have split thirty years prior to the convention and crafted a compelling narrative around Lincoln's rail-splitting hobby.

The splitting of rail would surely make Lincoln appear as an everyman.

He also knew he needed to put on a show that was entertaining to watch. If the nickname was presented in a lavish gesture full of intrigue and drama, he knew it would be cemented in people's minds. Hanks and Jennings barging on stage had caught everyone's attention. The rail-splitter image was born and white male voters connected with Lincoln's new rags-to-riches persona.

Why were convention attendees and delegates so quick to believe the story? Propaganda may have been commonplace at the time, but still, why did no one question the validity of his rail splitting background? Fact-checking speeches may have been a novel concept in the 1860s, but the line between truth and lie was not.

A story, if entertaining and presented in a compelling way, can convince anyone of anything.

Lincoln famously admitted he was not a fan of stage tricks but accepted the tag regardless. Of course, the story was not a complete falsehood. Lincoln had cut many rails, but axe work was far from consequential to his life.

Conjuring up images through personal stories and stretching the truth to win over the hearts and minds of the people is a practice as old as time.

Due to the rise in digital and social media, we are witnessing a surge in personal narratives told through user-generated content. Of course, the appeal of human stories is far from new.

Centuries before Lincoln's supporters pulled their stunt in Chicago, the authors of the Bible were writing gory stories about life, death, and resurrection: David and Goliath, John the Baptist, Adam and Eve.

These stories were personal and vivid for a reason: they were meant to convey lessons that would resonate with people, embedded so deeply in a collective consciousness that they could not be forgotten.

According to the Society of Biblical Literature (SBL), "Biblical stories aim to affect the reader, and we know they have succeeded when they stick with us. Eve chooses wisdom over Paradise and is expelled from the Garden of Eden. Cain kills Abel, whose blood cries out from the ground to accuse him. Abraham prepares to sacrifice his son at God's request. The Egyptian-raised Moses becomes the greatest prophet of ancient Israel."[5]

Epic narratives are typical across religious text, and we tend to believe the lessons in these stories because we see our thoughts, emotions, and lived experiences reflected in the texts.

"Our brains seem uniquely adapted to making sense of experience through stories. We tell stories and listen to them not just in our daily conversation but on the news, in the movies, and novels," Adriane Leveen writes for SBL.

Stories centered on human experience helped the authors of the Bible spread their message.

Let's consider the historical context in which the first five books of the Old Testament (Genesis, Exodus, Leviticus, Numbers, and Deuteronomy) were written. It helps explain why the books are full of horrific yet artfully entertaining stories.

The period 600–500 BC was a time of oral storytelling. Most people did not read and write. No one truly knows the motives in writing the books that encompass the Old Testament. But one could understand why a story of murder and revenge

---

5   Adriane Leveen, "Storytelling in the Bible," Society of Biblical Literature, accessed January 12, 2021.

would spread easily. The authors knew they had to write in a compelling and easy way to remember the style. Highbrow or technical prose would not provide an emotional hook for their desired audience—the people.[6]

In the book of Genesis, Cain and Abel were the two oldest sons of Adam and Eve. Both made sacrifices to the Lord, but Abel was favored. Cain killed his brother out of jealousy. The scene contains numerous lessons around lying, jealousy, and confession.

The authors of the book made a conscious effort to explain their teachings by *showing* instead of *telling*—a now common practice in the world of journalism. Telling someone not to be jealous is far less powerful than showing them what jealousy can do to a person.

They decided to teach these lessons through the experiences of Cain and Abel because they knew (as Oglesby knew) human stories have the power to cut through logic and go straight to our emotions.

Religion is not the only genre that has taken advantage of the tool of human storytelling.

Switching gears entirely, consider the Bravo reality TV series *The Real Housewives.*

The media franchise has gone from a small docuseries to a guilty pleasure with worldwide ratings. At first glance, the

---

6   Michael White, "Importance of the Oral Tradition," PBS, published April 1998.

reality pitch seems like an unlikely juggernaut. Who would want to watch the lives of privileged upper-class women from affluent suburbs shop in Gucci and Louis Vuitton stores and throw wine on each other? Well, apparently millions of people do.

The media franchise has amassed millions of followers and has spun off numerous shows for Bravo.

In 2016 *The Real Housewives of Atlanta* was the fifth-most watched TV series on cable television with 3.66 million viewers, beating out scripted blockbuster hits like *Westworld* and *South Park*. Of the fourteen total franchises, nine are based in the United States. Two are in California, including Beverly Hills and Orange County, with others scattered across the country in Dallas, Texas; Potomac, Maryland; and Atlanta, Georgia.[7]

Altogether, the series grosses millions of dollars in revenue for Bravo while also generating independent wealth for each housewife. In the show, they often hock their latest ventures such as clothing brands and fragrance companies and then take to social media and create UGC to help with promotion. Karen Huger, longtime star of *The Real Housewives of Potomac*, launched La'Dame, an eponymous perfume line named after her self-styled title in the show. *The Real Housewives of New York* mainstay LuAnn de Lesseps even launched an off-Broadway cabaret called *#CountessAndFriends* (in which she is the self-described "Countess of New York"), which she

---

7   Statista Research Department, "Leading cable TV series in the United States in Fall 2016, by number of viewers," Statista Database, published September 19, 2016.

promoted across her social media channels. The cabaret was so popular that even the events giant Live Nation signed de Lesseps to a multi-show deal for a national tour.

We are truly obsessed with watching everyday people on television (and online) simply living their lives.

Why? Why can't we turn away from the seemingly mundane, inconsequential drama?

I offer up one simple conclusion: because the problems in the women's lives reflect our own. We can see ourselves in the stars' emotional journeys, and that distracts from our own lives' obstacles. While we don't have millions of dollars or multiple homes, there's something about connecting with these people through their emotional struggles (which may be similar to our own) that makes what is otherwise unattainable somehow feel within reach. President Trump has a similar power. If we feel he is on our team and he tells us we are just like him, then maybe we can be as rich and powerful as him someday.

Seventeen percent of viewers between the ages of twenty-five and thirty-four say they watch the show because, "It helps [them] forget about real issues in [their] life/in the world."[8] If we focus on the lives of Karen and LuAnn, we can forget, for a moment, the problems in our lives.

This psychological effect is also induced by political entertainment and can possibly help explain Trump's victory in 2016.

---

8   Julia Stoll, "Reasons for watching reality TV in the United States as of March 2017, by age," Statista Database, published on Jan 27, 2021.

In the current age, there is a proliferation of individual storytelling due to the rise of new media platforms like Facebook, Instagram, and Twitter. But it's important to remember storytelling is far from new; it's simply the power to tell our own stories through UGC that is novel. We are now all the authors, editors, producers, and publishers.

The story of Abraham Lincoln as a rail splitter and the story of Cain and Abel in the Bible are just a few historical examples of the way human-focused narratives have been used as a tool to influence society.

As humans, we have always loved storytelling and personal stories. And now there is a proliferation of stories because of the new tools that allow us to share our lives more widely and readily.

These tools to create and share stories is what's new, and even scary.

How are we going to wield these powerful tools in society as they expand? That is the question I aim to explore in this book.

CHAPTER 2

PRINCIPLES OF AUTHENTIC STORYTELLING

———

Marketing is no longer about the stuff that you make, but about the stories you tell.

SETH GODIN

We're in an age of stories. Never before has it been easier to create and share simple, short, easy-to-consume stories about yourself. Our iPhones have turned us into photographers. Twitter has forced us to be pithier writers. Web and graphic software like Squarespace and Figma have turned us into visual designers.

Don't get me wrong; there will always be artists in creative fields that specialize and hone their craft for years. But the truth is the barriers to entry into many creative fields have been greatly reduced. Technology has democratized the creative storytelling process, which I believe is a net positive for society.

That being said, the effects of these new digital media technologies and platforms have, of course, attributed to a rise in noise and vitriol on the internet, which we can't—and shouldn't—ignore.

Take movements like QAnon and the Proud Boys. These groups have spread like wildfire thanks to subcommunities on social media. They've been able to tap into a very real and understandable skepticism about the state of our world, a skepticism that, to a degree, many of us have shared in 2020. But ultimately, fringe digital movements are just that. They are loud enough to garner media attention. But they are in the minority, which is why I think it important to focus on the positive outcomes of the new media-tech ecosystem we currently live in.

Before I get too far, it's worth spending a little time on how I am defining a few key terms in this book.

Storytelling can be an insubstantial word; its meaning is dulled by overuse. It's thrown around frequently in job descriptions and can sound vague or abstract. For the sake of this book, I am mostly referring to storytelling in the context of marketing. Storytellers can of course be found across media, in writers, designers, video directors, and musicians. But the digital boom has given us the tools to become more adept storytellers. We write posts, photograph our daily lives, and spend time telling the world about often mundane minutiae. We filter our lives in 280-character narratives. While this is distinctly separate from the kind of entertainment-style storytelling we watch in Hollywood films or read in publications like the *New Yorker*, it is storytelling nonetheless.

When I say *personal narrative*, I'm referring to the ability to craft your own story and mold a viewer's perceptions of you. This does not mean a personal narrative must necessarily talk about one's life or contain personal anecdotes. Rather, a personal narrative conveys the emotions, views, or opinions of a creator, often shared to strategically shape an audience's opinion. While viewers may learn something about the life and the perspective of the narrator, a personal narrative does not have to offer a glimpse into the life of the narrator. This is worth noting as I use Trump as a critical case study for what I call *nefarious storytellers* (creators who aim to distort reality). And Trump famously offers little vulnerability or insight when talking about his businesses or family.

But we do hear in his tweets a voice that sounds authentic and forces you to have an opinion about his personality.

"Despite the negative press covfefe," Trump tweeted in 2017.

"I don't believe the four Congresswomen are capable of loving our Country. They should apologize to America (and Israel) for the horrible (hateful) things they have said. They are destroying the Democrat Party, but are weak & insecure people who can never destroy our great Nation!" he tweeted in 2019.

His content is about his likes and his dislikes, especially his dislikes and the people he disdains, from Hillary Clinton to John McCain. But we do not hear anything that sounds authentic about his upbringing or his wife and son Baron. Though he cannot stand aside to narrate even brief moments of his own life (as most of us do through social media), he uses narrative focused on defying conformity to evoke emotional responses and draw in larger audiences.

User-generated content (UGC) is another important term I use throughout this text. In tech marketing we often use the term user-generated content in terms of generating awareness around new products or services. But the term is also intrinsically linked to personal narrative. UGC is defined as any form of content (copy, photography, videos) posted by an individual to their online platform as opposed to content posted by a business, brand, or organization. UGC is posted by people. UGC can be an Instagram story about how you got to work or a Medium post about how you got divorced. This category of content often cultivates emotional responses. UGC is also commonly used in journalism to crowdsource reporting.[9] It's a critical new phenomenon (at least in the digital space) that bears heavy weight across business, politics, and culture. UGC can help sell a new piece of software, land you a TV show deal, or spark a violent revolution. Crafting user-generated content is one of the most defining new activities of the twenty-first century. And it is becoming more important as the world of content gets noisier. UGC is becoming the quintessential way those in positions of power seek to demonstrate their authenticity, cut through the clutter, and reach their desired audience.

---

9   Katie Van Syckle, "Why the Times Crowdsources Reporting," The New York Times, July 19, 2018.

How is authentic narrative connected to UGC?

In *Fox Populism: Branding Conservatism as Working Class*, Reece Peck says, "The clutter created by the greater inclusion of sound bites, video imagery, and graphics in television newscasts beginning in the 1970s and 1980s only heightened television news' reliance on the cohering function of narrative." I go a step further to add that the dynamic visual editing power now accessible across social platforms like TikTok and Facebook have made narrative told through UGC essential in our day-to-day lives. Today content is more compelling because stories are more emotional. UGC is how we see the world and how we show the world who we are.

Peck also notes, "Narrative structures do more than make information intelligible. They carry tacit moral ideas and normative assumption about how the world *should* be."[10] Personal narratives are inherently subjective and biased.

Digital revolution is also a vague term that deserves some grounding. Walter Isaacson's *The Innovators: How a Group of Inventors, Hackers, Geniuses, and Geeks Created the Digital Revolution* is a sprawling 488-page historical analysis of the evolution of technology starting roughly in the 1830s. I use the term *digital revolution* quite differently. I loosely interchange "new media," "digital revolution," and "tech boom" to refer to our growing interdependence on specifically media technology today. These terms are meant to describe how social media is increasingly playing the role that broadcast TV once played for baby boomers for millennials and Gen Zers who have grown

---

10   Reece Peck, Fox Populism, (New York: Cambridge University Press, 2019) 79.

up as digital natives. I also refer to these terms to highlight the growth in various digital storytelling formats: podcasts, videos, animations, and, of course, the written word.

The way I've come to the above conclusions largely stems from my professional work in advertising, consulting, and brand marketing.

I started at IBM as a content director in 2017. In my first few months, I quickly realized executives had a common joke they would tell younger employees.

"What does IBM stand for?" they would ask snickering.

"International Business Machine," we would respond nervously, overthinking the question.

The executives would laugh back, "International Brotherhood of Magicians!"

We were left puzzled as they patted themselves on the back.

IBM has always had a renowned culture of design and storytelling. Thomas J. Watson historically declared in a 1973 lecture at the University of Pennsylvania, "Good design is good business."[11]

IBM's iconic secondary logo created by famous designer Paul Rand—an eye, a bee, and eight horizontal bars in the shape of an M—is a strong representation of its emphasis on design. The company has continued to build on that design heritage by

---

11   Staff, "Good Design Is Good Business," IBM Icons in Progress Blog.

hiring other heavy hitters like Mike Abbink. In 2017, Abbink launched the firm's first-ever bespoke font, IBM Plex.[12]

Between 2012 and 2017 the firm's revenue dropped by over 20 percent from $105.5 billion to $79.1 billion.[13] In response, IBM leadership not only doubled down on design, but also made a concerted effort to put more resources into marketing. Leadership launched new creative disciplines like IBM Originals, the team on which I sat, which was in charge of most original brand content storytelling.

I was a member of IBM Originals from 2017–2020. The department, originally launched in 2015, is in charge of content creation efforts across all lines of business in the multinational corporation. The team's mantra was, "Make less, matter more," a nod to the ever-noisy world of digital content.

IBM launched the new group after realizing storytelling was a powerful tool to bring in new business. It could no longer house a small team of advertisers in its corporate offices to do traditional sixty-second spots on TV. The firm needed a dedicated group that sat inside each of the IBM businesses to support marketing and advertising across the corporation.

At the start of the twenty-first century, we started to become overwhelmed with noise as Twitter and Facebook became more ubiquitous. Content was everywhere. We were bombarded with an ever-increasing number of photos, videos,

---

12   Anne Quito, "IBM has freed itself from the tyranny of Helvetica," Quartz, November 10, 2017.

13   James W. Cortada, IBM: The Ride and Fall and Reinvention of a Global Icon. Hardback Edition. (Cambridge, MA: MIT Press, 2019) 368.

and posts on our feeds. Brands were just creating to create without a solid strategy. And consumers are just as guilty of adding to the noise. IBM Originals was created in a direct response to that rise in digital and social creation.

IBM charged the Originals team with implementing a structure to reign in what the firm put out into digital the world, building a process for social and digital channels.

In a world where sponsored posts and banner ads compete to get noticed, the goal was to stand out by creating more attention-grabbing content through human-first stories.

IBM Originals pioneered a custom content creation process called, perhaps a bit uninspiringly, the IBM Content Model (or colloquially the "3x3x3," which referred to the distinct timelines for each set of content briefs).

The model consisted of many different components, but at its core were nine steps:

1. Input Brief: a long document (sometimes over twenty pages) that includes the essential background information you need to begin developing content.

2. Content strategy: documents how you use content to achieve your business objectives.

3. Concept brief: translates the insights from the input brief into creative fuel. It jump-starts the creative thinking that will build a bridge between business objectives and audience truths.

4. SWAT: a brainstorm session with a group of creative people to generate concepts that achieve your objective.

5. Green light: a meeting held with key stakeholders to review final concepts and gain agreement on the concept you'll proceed with into production.

6. Content plan: a plan that expands your creative concept into a story, identifies the assets to be built to tell that story in market, and asset briefs to begin asset production.

7. Asset brief: the specific details needed for each asset to begin production.

    a. Format

    b. Type

    c. Budget

    d. Timeline

8. Production: production of all content.

9. Go live session: a meeting with key stakeholders to review all content before it goes live.

This was the process to launch any new content-driven marketing campaign at IBM. Some steps took a few weeks and others a few months. For legacy employees who were used to doing things a certain way, implementing the process ruffled a lot of feathers.

Building a new way of working across a 300,000-person organization was no small undertaking.

"Why are we doing this?"

"What a waste of money."

At every corner, we experienced pushback for implementing this new process. When we succeeded, we were able to launch pieces like new books and documentaries, assets that no other brand in our space was creating and pieces of content we believed bolstered the IBM brand.

At other times, executives simply put a stop to our projects mid-production by pulling our funding.

Regardless, the IBM Originals team believed in the importance of a new kind of storytelling procedure. With the support of passionate and protective managers, we pushed on.

At every step of the IBM Content Model, the audience was our focus. What are they thinking? What are they feeling? Why would our customers pause and stop scrolling to watch a piece of content from an old server company like IBM? Working at a Fortune 500 company, we had the luxury of big budgets and fancy editing tools, but ultimately that wasn't what made our work stand out. We realized early on we needed to humanize the brand. IBM is old and big; we needed to make it less so. We needed to make personal connections with our audience by enhancing our narrative approach to storytelling.

So, we adopted story arcs that focused on people and emotions, not products we were selling. For example, in 2018 we shot a short film in Colombia about how an analytics-based solution transformed the livelihoods of local coffee farm owners. The film focused on the impact of the solution on the farmers, not the solution itself.

A common storytelling model we often used at IBM is called Monroe's motivated sequence.[14] Monroe's motivated sequence, traditionally used in speechwriting, is a persuasive structure designed to capture attention, expose a problem, introduce a solution, showcase a vision, and compel the viewer to action. The story arc looks like this:

Monroe's Motivated Sequence

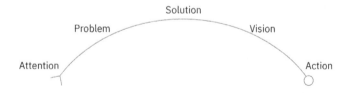

Our team used this structure to write blogs, produce video scripts, and even structure a book.

Another common story arc we used is the hero's journey. Some say there are seven stages to the hero's journey template;

---

14 Eric Robertson, "Monroe's Motivated Sequence | COMMUNICATION STUDIES," May 10, 2019, 16:23 minutes.

others argue there are three. For the sake of simplicity, think about a common narrative I'm sure you've seen before in movies or TV shows.

A lonely hero tries to find themself. A sudden and unexpected journey promising adventure and peril follows. A test of character, strength, and skill ensues. An ultimate battle that tests the hero's resolve comes about. And the triumphant return home of the hero occurs.[15]

The hero's journey is everywhere: *Star Wars*, "The Gingerbread Man," *The Lion King*, *To Kill a Mockingbird*. It's one of the most commonly used story templates throughout history.

And there are countless more story arcs we used at IBM to help inspire our human-first storytelling process, like Duarte's sparkline and the rags-to-riches arc.

Filmmaker Kurt Vonnegut is credited with pinning down the Cinderella and "from bad to worse" arcs, which I've also adapted for personal projects.[16]

Storytelling is obviously not new, nor are many stories truly original. But storytelling has been made more accessible over time. We simply use what inspired us and adapt that for what we want to say. The IBM Content Model was innovative from a corporate business-to-business (B2B) perspective, but the

---

15 "Writing 101: What Is the Hero's Journey? 2 Hero's Journey Examples in Film," Masterclass (blog), Oct 2, 2020.

16 Jon Fusco, "The 6 Emotional Arcs of Storytelling, Why You Should Use Them, and Which One is Best," No Film School (blog), November 29, 2016.

model was put together by picking and choosing aspects of storytelling processes that have been around for a long time.

Realizing there was a starting point in the storytelling process was a major turning point in my own creative professional journey.

I used to think "storytelling" was a fluffy word. In the first few years of my marketing career, I heard it and saw it in job descriptions everywhere. I would constantly ask myself, "What does that actually mean?"

It took nine years working in marketing and advertising—and harsh editors and executive creative directors—to make it real for me.

Though there are no rules to being a good storyteller, there are some common themes: strong sense of narrative, using known tropes, containing some showmanship, crafting with empathy always top of mind, being knowledgeable about various story constructions, building trust, and even knowing how to coach. But perhaps uniquely relevant to today's digital landscape is understanding how to be agile and nimble with your approach to story.

Seth Godin—a prominent businessman, marketer, and TED speaker—is an expert in storytelling. He believes a great storyteller can connect with audiences on a personal level and provide a sense of reaffirmation.

"Great stories agree with our worldview. The best stories don't teach people anything new. Instead, the best stories agree with what the audience already believes and makes the members of the audience feel smart and secure when reminded how right they were in the first place."[17]

We're all looking for validation. One aspect of being a good storyteller is being able to tap into that human nature and make the viewer feel at ease. Make them feel like they are among good company. Given the rise of digital media, that's increasingly been the case. We live in digital bubbles of our own making. Our feeds become self-fulfilling prophecies because we are in charge of who we follow. This has led to the phenomenon of the echo chamber.

Part of the reason the political left was so caught off guard by Trump's unexpected 2016 victory was the fact that we tend to pay attention to stories we agree with personally and not just stories from institutional news media outlets like CNN or Fox News. Since the individual is given the tools to be a better storyteller, we're now more swayed by friends and family who post frequently.

So, where's the hope? Is the proliferation of storytelling platforms and UGC a net positive for society? I think the hope is that if we can tell stories well, we can connect to individuals while also helping them see the shared experiences across lines of differences. We have an opportunity to understand those different from ourselves better.

Pinning down just what makes a storyteller strong is tough. But there is no doubt we are all storytellers simply due to the

---

17   Seth Godin, "Ode: How to tell a great story," Seth Godin (blog), April 27, 2006.

fact that we are all active on social media. We must be wary of this newfound power. Now that stories are a mass commodity, we must be more cautious consumers of content. But if we are able to be cautious and purposeful with our creation and consumption of UGC, we can connect with communities and individuals outside our comfort zone.

CHAPTER 3

THE POWER OF OWNING YOUR STORY

———

My dad is a tall Punjabi man who wears a turban and is a bit heavyset.

I have a complicated relationship with my father. My parents divorced when I was twelve, and he became a distant figure in my life when my mother and I moved out of the house to start over in an adjacent town. He routinely blamed her for the separation and I, like many children of divorce, often found myself in the middle of contentious communication, unsure of exactly what role I was supposed to play.

In adulthood, my father and I have attempted to mend our relationship. In this newfound, albeit tentative, camaraderie, I've seen the ways in which his personal life story served as a tool in building his business and securing a place in his community. He's always been loud and extroverted about his experience weaving through American society as an Indian immigrant, but it wasn't until recently that I came to understand why he put so much emphasis on his heritage and ethnicity.

My dad is the American dream incarnate. He came to the United States in 1972 with little money in his pocket and a commitment to build a life for himself and my mother. He started working in car dealerships as a salesman, ultimately earning a management position in a small dealership in Fresno County, California.

Eventually, he and my mother saved enough so that he could buy and run his own dealership. Over time that dealership became so successful he was able to buy another, and then another. He ended up running a small empire of dealerships (General Motors, Chevrolet, Subarus, Suzukis, and others) across Southern California before retiring in 2017.

Throughout his fifty years in the States, he fell in love with his work—not necessarily with cars, but the small business itself. He devoted himself to the nuts and bolts of running an enterprise, invigorated by the intricacies of making it work. However, with his success (and broad influence in the towns and cities where he operated) came discrimination and often intense racism (sometimes even death threats). Rather than attempt to hide the things for which he was targeted, he chose to use what made him different to his advantage.

The way he talked about growing up in India and his experience coming to the United States as an immigrant—*that* is what won people over.

The story of immigrants from humble beginnings with a strong work ethic is one often told in the United States. However, I believe it bears repeating as it is easy for people like myself to take for granted the liberties and opportunities afforded to us simply by virtue of where we are born. "When I came to this country, I had nothing. My parents were poor, and there were no opportunities in India," my father often said when sharing his story with employees, customers, or partners. With this statement he was able to illustrate much more than he said—a commitment to hard work, an ability to imagine and realize a better future, and a belief in the opportunity America can afford to some (though too often not all) of its citizens. He was able to build trust, deepen connections, and reveal some part of his character by sharing his story. The narrative he told not only invested others in his success, but also invited the listener to share in it.

And for what it's worth, his story is one to tell. He and my mother entered into an arranged marriage in 1970 in North India. He came to the United States and worked for two years without her to earn enough money to fly her to California.

Growing up, I remember him regaling us with long monologues about his experiences in the Indian Navy or illustrating a point via anecdotes from his own upbringing when he didn't have much money. As his son, I often felt like I was listening to a rambling lecture, caught somewhere between a stream of consciousness and professorial circumlocution. He always had a point, but it often seemed like he could take forever to make it. However, I've since come to understand his eagerness to tell his story in a different context.

Since arriving in America, my father has stood out. When you're not white, your perceived racial identity and religious signifiers are what people see first. As a turban-wearing brown man with a long white beard, my father has felt compelled to explain his existence to a world that does not readily accept him. If his physical identifiers were the basis on which many would choose to reject him—or worse, persecute him—then his story was how he would win them over.

One of my earliest recollections of this was on a business trip to Puerto Rico in 1999.

As we often did, my mom and I tagged along for my father's conference. During his time off, we would hang out by the pool or go sightseeing. On this occasion, we were walking in a shopping mall when a group of young boys stopped and stared at him. They were my age (around eleven), and I was petrified, desperately wanting to be accepted, or at least unnoticed. As they took us in, their eyes widened, and they started to point and shout comments: "Terrorist!" "Are you related to Osama bin Laden?" and "Why are you wearing that weird thing on your head?" It felt like they were circling as the words surrounded us.

My dad smiled and politely greeted them, and we walked away. To my surprise, he seemingly paid no mind to any of it. I, on the other hand, was mortified. Being a vulnerable, fragile teenager, I didn't want to walk around with my dad anymore because I was embarrassed by how he looked and the attention it brought to us or—perhaps more to the point—to me. Part of me thinks he realized that, for which I feel immensely guilty, but we never really talked about it.

Teenage boys are the worst.

I have always wondered how experiences like the one in Puerto Rico affected him. I know he went through worse, but, like many Asian parents, he never wanted to discuss his feelings. What I observed was that he absorbed the blows life gave him and used them to his advantage.

He brought those stories into the workplace, illustrating that while you can't control other people's politeness, treating others with respect and patience are always in your control. When speaking to his team, he was an immigrant speaking to a room full of immigrants. Many of my dad's employees were Mexican and Salvadoran, and the unfortunate reality is that they all dealt with racism of various severity levels. To hear those stories from your boss must have not only been powerful but extremely reassuring—a sort of confirmation that you're not alone.

His stories—the lessons he pulled from his own life experiences—connected directly with anyone who had ever felt different. The empathy and understanding he conveyed allowed him to develop strong business relationships that bolstered his success.

My father is obsessed with status and the ways in which society views successful people. There weren't many paths for Sikh men in America to follow, so he carved his own. When he made enough money to purchase a large dealership in Riverside, California, a midsize, blue-collar town in inland California, he wanted to join a country club. Upon receiving his application, the board asked him to come in for an in-person interview to see if he was a good fit. After sitting and talking for a while, the board was on its way to accepting him as a member. At the last moment, one of the board members said in all seriousness, "Singh, you know you'll have to take off the hat when you're at the club."

Turbans were not exempt from the clubs no-hat policy. My dad responded, "The turban is a part of my religion. I am a Sikh. And it is a sign of respect to God." As he did to the boys in Puerto Rico, he smiled, thanked the board for their time, and walked out.

The board didn't budge and rejected his application.

Of the experience, he would say, "You have to stick to what you believe in and not change for anyone," and, "You must meet hate with courtesy and respect—never anger." He ended up joining a different country club. After hearing the story many of the immigrant and minority club members left the racist club and followed him to the other. Over the year he would create lifelong bonds with many employees and business partners who shared experiences of marginalization in a white male–dominated society.

That ability to take an experience and make it your own was something I realized had immense impact.

In 2014, I moved to Washington, DC, excited, wide eyed, and naive. Like many millennials in DC during the Obama administration, I wanted to save the world and felt I knew exactly how to do it.

As a college student and Fulbright Scholar, I focused on foreign policy and international relations. As an Indian American, I regularly felt I was being pulled in two directions, and the foreign policy community embraced this duality.

It was a comfortable home for someone like me. It's an industry in which having multiple identities was not only commonplace but also respected.

My first job was at a think tank called the Aspen Institute. I was an assistant editor and public affairs associate in the communications department. Everyone who worked there was well credentialed and brilliant—or so their titles made one think. In every corner of the office, there was a director or vice president of a major policy issue. As a junior employee and new arrival to the DC political arena, I was intimidated and eager to prove myself. I copyedited long reports, helped put together numerous community book talks, and even got two articles published with my byline.

The organization was structured by policy area. There was a national security team, justice and civic identity team, sports and society team, and so on. Teams operated in silos, and it was rare they crossed paths on projects or events, aside from the hallmark Aspen Ideas Festival each year. Outside of the weeklong festival in Colorado, the only real thing that tied us all together was the logo: a blue Aspen leaf.

As I got to know people outside of my team, it seemed there was one other common experience at the Aspen Institute: a constant feeling of panic and stress. Despite success and growth within the organization, after a few months in what proved to be a toxic work environment, I quit.

"So, I hear you're leaving," my boss said.

"Yes, but I've had such an amazing experience. I'm so lucky to have gotten the opportunity to work here," I said.

"Well, you weren't that good of a writer anyway. You probably would have lasted another month or so."

The comment blindsided me. Our working relationship had been overwhelmingly positive, and I had not expected the exit interview to be confrontational. I certainly had not anticipated that my boss, who hired me and proactively supported my development, would call my qualifications into question. With hindsight, I can understand the pressures a manager is under to retain staff and that manager–employee relationships can feel personal. But at the time, all I felt was frustration that he had made me feel guilty for leaving a job I hated.

I found myself talking about that exit interview frequently with other young writers and marketing types in DC who just starting out in journalism, media, marketing, or communications. Many of us had experiences with similar managers whether on Capitol Hill, think tanks, or NGO offices. Ultimately, this miserable experience helped me form long-lasting professional relationships.

Throughout my dad's life, he's been able to identify what experience he could tell stories about to help him succeed.

You can always see yourself in a story you love. When my dad speaks about his past, he invites you to step into his shoes and experience what he experienced. The power of his story sparked my own.

CHAPTER 4

MY JOURNEY INTO STORYTELLING

———

*To the world you may be one person, but to
one person you may be the world.*

DR. SEUSS

At age twenty-four, I had an existential crisis. I had just quit my job at the Aspen Institute and had no idea what I wanted to do next.

I knew I wanted to do something that gave me purpose—a role that made me feel I was helping to make the world a better place. But I had no idea what that looked like, paralyzed by what felt were an endless number of possible paths.

In an effort to move forward, I shifted my mindset towards identifying the tangible skills I wanted to perfect. What did I want to be good at? With a liberal arts education, I was okay at a lot of things, but not especially good at any one.

I started freelance writing when I moved to DC. At first, it was just a way to make some extra cash while job hunting.

But I quickly realized it meant much more to me. Writing was both professional and personal. It was how I processed what was happening in my life and in the world at large.

Over the next nine years, I fell in love with writing.

From Booz Allen Hamilton, a strategy and defense consulting firm in Washington, DC, to IBM in New York City, I worked on video scripts, speeches, podcasts, storyboards, and web/social/ad copy. I even once wrote a preventative health brochure for soldiers in Afghanistan that provided hand-washing instructions (little did I know how relevant that would come to be). They weren't all my favorite projects, but the wide range helped me realize you didn't need to write novels or TV scripts to be a writer.

In those years, I came to believe deeply in the power of personal stories to influence our decisions. Stories that center around humanity connect to our core beliefs. That's been true for centuries but bears repeating as UGC has become a daily occurrence in our lives.

I witnessed this through an inconsequential marketing project called "Booz Allen Big Ideas." As part of the initiative, I had the opportunity to interview Thad Allen, the former head of the US Coast Guard.

Allen is a formative presence. He's tall (maybe around 6'3") and a little heavy set, with broad shoulders. He speaks in a deep voice with an incredibly serious tone. He looks and sounds like a war hero straight out of central casting. And he has a résumé to match. Just a few of the notable milestones in his life include running America's response efforts to Hurricane Katrina in Louisiana in 2005 and managing response and cleanup of the Deepwater Horizon oil spill in 2010.

The interview was for a podcast profiling Booz Allen executives. The project was meant to highlight managerial lessons from military veterans, and we focused our interview on his work with FEMA while responding to Hurricane Katrina. America's response to the disaster was, of course, controversial.[18] Many argued there were issues with management teams, which is what I thought we'd discuss.

To my surprise, the interview turned toward the emotional intelligence required to navigate the situation on the ground in the aftermath of the hurricane.

"You're dealing with a wide array of emotions when responding to a natural disaster like Katrina. You have to have empathy and understanding for every stakeholder. You may not always agree with them. And they may not be able to properly respond due to their distress. But you have to understand the intensity of their feelings. You can't negate their emotions," Allen said.

"To be able to properly do that when interacting and working with such a wide range of emotions you have to work on

18   Valerie Bauerlein, "Lessons Learned From the Response to Katrina's Havoc," Wall Street Journal, August 28, 2015.

your own emotional intelligence. In my own case, I've been working on that over a lifetime. And that's what gave me the ability to actually see other people's points of view, and effectively aggregate them all together to figure out a course to effectively respond to the crisis. If I didn't do that, I would have ended up making different groups of people from state and local government feel disenfranchised."

Once released, the profile made its way across the usual internal and external marketing channels at Booz, but the shelf life of content is short. It soon quietly disappeared like many a niche corporate marketing campaign.[19] Three months later I received an email from a colleague. She said that a potential client had referenced the podcast interview, citing it as the primary factor in her decision to proceed with the firm. It had made her feel like she could trust the company. Of course, she knew she wouldn't be working with Thad personally, but she thought if people like him were at Booz Allen, she'd be in good hands.

Certainly, Thad Allen had not shared his story with the intent of winning Booz Allen new business, but this was a more than welcome outcome: it was confirmation of the power of personal storytelling. Allen's own voice was ultimately more compelling than any tagline touting the firm's trustworthiness that our team could have come up with. It was authentic and raw. It was not an overproduced advertisement or quote in a pamphlet. Perhaps the client was a veteran or grew up in New Orleans. Maybe she saw her own values reflected in

19 Karam Sethi, "Emotional Intelligence and Empathy for Effective Leadership with Thad Allen," Booz Allen Big Ideas Podcast. October 11, 2015.

his story or connected to his introspection. Whatever it was, Allen resonated with her.

Of course, Allen's story was particularly powerful in large part because he was able to tell it himself. There was no script, and, within the confines of a loose interview structure, he spoke with great authenticity and vulnerability about his personal values.

One of the most important aspects of a successful story is authenticity. Stories are a mechanism for us to relate to and connect with people in the world around us. Personal narrative stories tell us there is someone else out there who gets it. If a storyteller is not able to look themselves in the mirror and truly know themself, they're likely to come off as inauthentic, diluting the power of their story.

In 2017, I participated in one of the most influential classes of my life at Columbia Business School called Leadership & Organization Change. During the class we took a qualitative and quantitative approach to personal development and learned about leadership from both personal and scientific perspectives. One of the most impactful aspects of the class was establishing a personal and professional values tree. It sounds a little hokey, but stay with me.

The value tree—a list of six to eight interpersonal values connected to one another—gave me a structure through which to face my personal and professional fears.

I've always had a deep fear of failure, and this fear was placed in my "excellence" value. I also contain a lot of insecurity around not being intelligent enough, which I placed in an "intellectualism" value. My fear of becoming too focused on profits and not enough on helping the world was placed in a value I called "supporting others."

These values were a way for me to address my fears head on.

By creating a structure to place my fears I could better understand them and in doing so better understand myself, which helped me move past numerous concerns on the road in my career. Like Allen talked about in the interview, growing my emotional intelligence was key to becoming a better writer and storyteller.

Writing has become a home for me. It is a role to which I am not only able but required to bring my whole self. I count myself lucky to have found that.

There are loads of resources to build your own values tree online, but here are a few of my favorites:

- "Inner Mastery. Outer Impact," a keynote talk by professor Hitendra Wadhwa at the Brand Minds conference in 2019;

- *Mindset: The New Psychology of Success*, a book by Carol S. Dweck; and

- *The Art of Learning: An Inner Journey to Optimal Performance*, a book by Josh Waitzkin.

There are also some great mental exercises to jumpstart thinking about your values. Here are two from my graduate school class I found useful:

EXERCISE 1

Think about a situation at work in which you felt angry or hurt. What's most important to you that was missing in that situation?

_____

Don't write what caused your anger or hurt. Write what is missing.

Respond with one word that describes the essence of your response to the question. Use a few words if you must. Only your definitions of the words and values you use are important. Dictionary definitions or other people's definitions are not relevant.

What else was missing?

_____

EXERCISE 2

Think about one of your most important current work situations or one from the recent past. Pick a situation that is very different in character than the first exercise above. Imagine yourself back in this situation.

What is most important about this situation to you, personally?

_____

Respond with one word that describes the essence of your response to the question. Use a few words if you must.

What else is important to you, personally?

_____

These are just starting points, but nonetheless useful when thinking about your own values tree.

CHAPTER 5

AUTHENTIC STORYTELLING AND THE FALL OF THE BRAND

———

"It's all about the brand."

That's probably something you've heard before. With the rise of digital technologies and social media, the ways in which businesses bring their brands to life in a digital world translate directly into the success for many companies.

But we are at a shaky point with our relationship with brands. For the past few decades, we have been obsessed with the story of companies pushing the boundaries of technology, such as Google, Facebook, Amazon, and Apple, among others. We attribute a large part of their success to their strong brand presence.

These companies have changed, and continue to change, the way we weave through society. We moved from desktops to laptops to smartphones overnight.

We started to connect with friends and family in other countries more frequently. But it's a double-edged sword, as we've also been bombarded with more ads for stuff we don't want. And we have yet to even skim the surface of the power of search, which makes information more accessible than ever before. The tech arms race is unfolding before our eyes.

With new and novel technologies came a boom in thrilling companies disrupting all types of industries. Throughout the first two decades of the twenty-first century, game-changing firms aimed at disrupting traditional industries sprouted up left and right. These have, of course, become household names: Casper, Airbnb, Uber, and the like. The power of the brand is often conveyed via personal narratives. Take Casper, the mattress start-up, for example.

The founders of Casper thought mattress shopping was outdated. So they decided to forgo expensive brick and mortar stores and sell directly to consumers via a website—the first business to ship a mattress in a box. Since the company's launch in 2014, a slew of competitors have followed their lead with direct-to-consumer mattresses. Casper's novel approach to brand—quizzes about sleep on subway ads and whimsical blogs about how to put your children to sleep more effectively—asked the consumer to rethink how we approach the common human experience of sleep. And they made the experience of receiving the product novel as well. Having predominantly grown up in cities, I was used to lugging a mattress across busy side streets or renting U-Hauls to retrieve new beds from Craigslist postings—but not with Casper. I was amazed when my Casper mattress arrived at my doorstep, neatly packaged in a well-designed box. All I had to do was simply unpack and unfold onto my box spring.

Airbnb is another great example of a company that was able to shake up a previously unshakable industry.

Hoteling has largely remained stagnant for decades. There was a time when persuading someone to sleep in another person's room instead of a freshly cleaned hotel bed would have been unthinkable. Airbnb, the house-sharing unicorn, changed that.

They invented a new way of experiencing travel solely by creating a novel kind of marketplace platform connecting homeowners with travelers.

And now they are worth $31 billion. When I travel with my family, we don't look for hotels on Hilton's or Westin's websites because we know we'll save money, have more space, and be surrounded by locals (instead of tourists) in homes listed on Airbnb.

These brands represent what many Americans believe to be true: we are destined to innovate and challenge the status quo. But the boom had to slow down eventually. We're starting to lose our affinity with these new and edgy brands. We're actually becoming disillusioned as many start-ups turn into traditional corporations.

But why? What could be more interesting to Americans than a booming start-up?

It's not necessarily the number of companies sprouting up that has made us bewildered, but the callousness and inauthenticity through which many new companies market themselves to the world.

The Big Tech hearings of the summer of 2020 provide a few clues. On July 29, 2020, the House Judiciary Antitrust Subcommittee brought the CEOs of Google, Facebook, Amazon, and Apple in to question them about their controversial business practices.

In an opinion piece featured in *Wired* magazine, Roger McNamee, author of *Zucked: Waking Up to the Facebook Catastrophe*, succinctly summarizes the hearings:

"Forty years of deregulation have given America's largest corporations the ability to impose their will on competitors, suppliers, customers, employees, and communities. The pandemic, the economic contraction, and the murder of George Floyd have combined to trigger a national conversation about values and priorities. The time to rebuild them has arrived."[20]

The tumultuous year of 2020 helped shed a spotlight on many troubling realities in the business community. But the key word in the quote above is "corporation." The small, scrappy start-ups that started in garages are no more. These giants have become institutions and ultimately synonymous with "the Man."

Scrutiny over tech CEOs had been happening for years, but seeing Mark Zuckerberg, Jeff Bezos, Sundar Pichai, and Tim Cook together on a virtual stage was a watershed moment.

The hearings held the person behind the brand accountable. That's a significant distinction because shaping a narrative

---

20 Roger McNamee, "A Primer to Big Tech's Antitrust Hearing: They're (Almost) All Guilty," Wired, July 24, 2020.

case around a person is very different than building a story around a brand.

During the opening testimonials, each CEO gave their five-minute story, including where they came from, how they rose to the top, and what their values are. Pichai, the CEO of Google and its parent company Alphabet, artfully walked through his story of growing up in India and how the accessibility of laptops both impressed and inspired him when he moved to the United States for graduate school. His rags-to-riches story is not a new one. It's a tale we, a country founded by immigrants, can identify with. His choice to tell that story, instead of one about the humble beginnings of Google the company, is also significant. The CEOs decided to make it personal rather than about the brand.

Why? Because it was the moment we started to care about people more than the brand. It was in that moment when I realized the individual stories of the leaders that represent the brand are more important than the brands themselves, as they have more influence over public opinion. It is the easiest lever for these leaders to pull in garnering sympathy for large corporations that many are frustrated with and feel have too much power. Former Uber CEO Travis Kalanick's story offers another good, albeit less flattering, example.

Kalanick's own story began far before founding Uber, the ride-sharing company, in 2009. But I'll fast-forward and focus on the story of his resignation as CEO in 2017.

According to an op-ed in the *New York Times*:

"Mr. Kalanick's troubles began earlier [in 2017] after a former Uber engineer detailed what she said was sexual harassment at the company, opening the floodgates for more complaints and spurring internal investigations."[21]

In addition to the numerous sexual assault allegations and public intoxication events that went viral on social media, his ties to the Trump administration added to the list of public misgivings that shape the story of the CEO. Ultimately, Uber's board of directors asked him to step down with the hope that his resignation would separate Kalanick from the Uber brand.

The shift in public awareness from brands to people is just beginning. We're at an inflection point due to the rise in UGC, and the personal narrative is only going to become more critical in culture, politics, and business.

A personal brand fueled by thoughtful UGC on your social media channels is no longer just nice to have; it's everything. But consumers should be wary of personal narratives eclipsing personal or professional irresponsibility. Uber's CEO is not the only nefarious storyteller trying to shape reality. The next two decades will look decidedly different than the past two in terms of how we shape perception in the public's eye.

As Kalanick and Pichai show us, the story of the people behind brands matters now more than ever before—whether you're a CEO, politician, or cultural icon. And just as critical to that personal story is authenticity as told through UGC. In a new

---

21   Mike Isaac, "Uber Founder Travis Kalanick Resigns as C.E.O.," The New York Times, September 19, 2017.

world of mass digital-content consumption, it's now easier for consumers to tell what's real and what's not.

After nine years in marketing, I've realized marketers (myself included) get restless during times of crisis. We need to feel we're getting our message out there and telling our stakeholders (investors, customers, clients) what we stand for. They're not immoral goals, but our execution tends to be tone deaf and can have mixed results.

During the 2017 Black Lives Matter protests, Pepsi launched a now infamous spot featuring Kendall Jenner.[22] Dressed in a bedazzled denim outfit, Jenner walks in front of Black Lives Matter protesters and hands a can of Pepsi to an intimidating police officer holding the line. The tense atmosphere immediately dissipates and everyone smiles. The soda product has solved systemic racism in our society. Meant to convey unity, the ad came off as incredibly oblivious, and the internet unanimously shunned the beverage company's attempt at centering themselves in a moment of social reckoning.

In 2018, Jack in the Box launched an ad to introduce new teriyaki bowls to its menus. In the sixty-second video, Jack pokes fun at the word "bowls" as a euphemism for male genitalia ("balls") in an attempt to make light of the #MeToo movement. Again, the internet was incensed. Many called the message insensitive and inappropriately timed. *AdWeek's* David Griner even called the commercial one of the most tone-deaf ads of the #MeToo era.

---

22 Yash Yadav, "Full Pepsi Commercial Starring Kendal Jenner," April 6, 2017, 2:48 minutes.

There are many more examples, but here is just one more.

From 2015–2018, rainbow flags also had a moment in the business marketing community. Corporations pushed out supportive LGBTQ+ messaging across social media channels and promoted their support of the non-cis community. But, like many forms of marketing, the line between support and profiteering was blurred.

A 2018 *Wired* article broke down the problem at the core of the trend. "Rainbow-washing allows people, governments, and corporations that don't do tangible work to support LGBTQ+ communities at any other time during the year to slap a rainbow on top of something in June and call it allyship," the piece reads.[23]

It's perfectly reasonable for corporations to not take a stance and just go about their business, but if they aren't going to help in a meaningful way, they shouldn't be trying to profit off a cause they don't truly care about. The marketing community often does more harm than good when we attempt to control, script, and force false narratives instead of being authentic to the businesses we represent. It's an understandable challenge.

Marketing departments at large corporations stand distinct from an enterprise's core business. At IBM, for example, marketing departments (with anywhere from eighteen to forty people) are allocated inside each line of business at the company. But our offices in New York City solely consist of marketing team members. So most, if not all, marketers have

---

23   Wired Staff, "LGBTQ Pride Consumerism," Wired, June 21, 2018.

little interaction with the business team members (consultants, product managers, general managers) we market to the world. This church and state separation also means marketing teams generally have little influence over tangible change inside large organizations.

The COVID-19 pandemic spurred another round of jumpiness amongst marketers at international brands. Emotive messaging meant to pull on consumer heartstrings has largely fallen flat and, on a few occasions, even deterred potential consumers. Smaller start-ups, however, have found meaningful ways of maintaining relevance in their market without sounding contrived. That's no small feat in a content-filled digital world.

Various forms of advertisements bombard consumers every day. According to eMarketer, the modern consumer is expected to spend 121.30 minutes per day watching digital video content in 2021.[24] The more video content is consumed, the less patience we have for ads we don't care about. The repercussion of a bad ad is no longer just a click of the "Skip Ads" button. Consumers are starting to distrust brands they perceive as fake.

The infamous marketing gaffe of McDonald's in 2020 is a prime example. In response to the tragic deaths of more than 258,000 worldwide due to COVID-19, the burger giant decided to show its solidarity by putting space in between its famous double arches. As a symbol of social distancing, this

---

24 Ethan Cramer-Flood, "US Average Time Spent per Day with Digital Video," eMarketer, February 4, 2020.

was meant to be a grand gesture of empathy—but McDonald's faced intense backlash.

US senator from Vermont Bernie Sanders even tweeted at the company telling them to give their employees paid sick leave instead of a rebranding project.

During the month of April, sales dropped dramatically for the burger giant. The company reported that same-store sales went down 3.4 percent while earnings per share fell below analysts' forecasts to $1.47.[25] Of course, much of the financial distress can be attributed to global lockdowns, but customers' attitudes were nonetheless tarnished by the gimmick. The company's Net Promoter Score, a common benchmark for customer brand loyalty, dropped to -8, indicating customers were not returning to COVID-safe drive-thrus.[26]

Insubstantial gestures aren't just making customers wince: they're being stored in consumers' brains as pockets of animosity. This is why authenticity in storytelling matters.

Though McDonald's is taking steps to remedy the mistake, the damage is done. And they're not alone.

Many big brands are fumbling storytelling in the midst of the pandemic. Within twenty-four hours, Adidas reversed their "stay open" order during the pandemic amidst intense backlash. KFC shut down an ad showing customers licking

---

25 Heather Haddon, "McDonald's Sales Fall as Coronavirus Pandemic Changes Dining Habits," Wall Street Journal, April 3, 2020.

26 Customer Guru, Net promoter Score, McDonalds.

unwashed hands in slow motion (a nod to the famous "finger lickin' good" tag line) launched in early 2020.

On the other end of the spectrum, we saw many start-ups approach the crisis by showing, not telling. Start-ups are inherently more adept at telling their story. Of course this is, in part, due to the fact that they are smaller and less complex operationally.

Solemates, a start-up focused on heel protectors and extension products, launched a "buy-one-give-one" campaign. For every unit purchased, the company will donate an antifriction balm that helps fight mask irritation to a frontline worker.

Headspace, a health care app focused on meditation, created a website full of resources to help with COVID-19 anxiety. They even started offering free access to their premium services for frontline healthcare workers: "Helping those who care for us, care for themselves."

Emilie Heathe, a boutique beauty brand, is donating 20 percent of its sales to GLAM4GOOD. The nonprofit delivers clothing, care packages, and PPE to frontline workers who cannot sleep at their homes (for fear of spreading the virus to loved ones).

Air Company, a vodka start-up that developed a process to use captured carbon dioxide to make liquor, shifted its production to making hand sanitizer for New York City communities.

SantM, a functional Italian footwear brand, and the Nemours Children's Hospital Network have teamed up to raise funds and produce thousands of face masks for the hospital.

These companies all have one thing in common: instead of rushing to create marketing fluff, they focused their attention and pivoted their operations to meet real needs. They created real change and told stories that represented the real aspects of their founders' values. That resulted in organic UGC that supported the brand.

Today, that's what we as consumers expect.

The challenge for marketing teams is that they're not usually set up to make enterprise-wide decisions at big corporations like McDonald's. It is much easier for the marketing departments of smaller companies to make big decisions when marketing decisions are made by the CEO, COO, and CMO sitting at the same table. At places like IBM and McDonald's, the upper echelon of the marketing department has a tight budget and has likely never interacted with executive leadership outside the chief marketing office.

But whether small or large, action is what resonates with consumers.

According to a recent study conducted by *Campaign*, 43 percent of millennials believe brands need to help during the pandemic.[27] Start-ups understand this and are proving they know the public will not tolerate inaction. Marketers should look to see what their followers and audiences do and align that to their UGC strategy.

---

27 Michael Heusner, "Millennials want brands to communicate more during COVID-19 crisis, study finds," Campaign, April 1, 2020.

"Hey. We're a Brand." A parody advertisement launched in 2020 by copywriter Samantha Geloso perfectly encapsulates the current branded-content moment.

In it, a fictional company takes viewers on an emotional journey through empty supermarkets and hospitals with forlorn patients in masks. In the end, viewers realize the company used melancholy music and woeful footage to guilt audiences into purchasing a product.

After being in the field for many years I can admit that I too, at the behest of bosses driven by sales and increased clicks, exaggerated stories to convert my viewers.

The crux of the problem is this: many of the ads we've been hit with in 2020 have been exploiting the genuine anxiety consumers feel today but without authentic empathy. And Geloso's film makes that all too clear.

In today's world, words must be met with action, and that action is told through UGC. That is to say, there is no story without real change.

Taking a pause and resisting the urge to react can sometimes be the hardest decision marketers make. Instead of inadvertently creating fires, marketers should take this moment to be thoughtful and ask themselves what matters to their teams, their leadership, and their customers. If now is not an opportune moment to ask yourself what you believe, when is?

CHAPTER 6

RISE OF PERSONAL NARRATIVE CONTENT

———

*It is this that makes people so willing to follow brash,
strong-looking demagogues with tight jaws and loud
voices: those who focus their measured words and
their sharpened eyes in the intensity of hate, and so
seem most capable of cleansing the world of the vague,
the weak, the uncertain, the evil. Ah, to give oneself
over to their direction—what calm, what relief.*

ERNEST BECKER, THE BIRTH AND DEATH

OF MEANING: AN INTERDISCIPLINARY

PERSPECTIVE ON THE PROBLEM OF MAN

"Trump connected with Wisconsin on a personal level. I'm
from Wisconsin. I know these people. That's how he won.
It makes me want to vomit, but he *was* the guy you wanted
to get a beer with," Ben Royce, professor of data and storytelling at Columbia University, said during an interview
we had in 2020.

Six states switched from Democrat to Republican from 2012–2016: Iowa, Michigan, Ohio, Pennsylvania, Florida, and Wisconsin, each with very similar chances of swinging either way. While interviewing Professor Royce, he offered a clear take on how our forty-fifth president won in 2016.

There were many significant events that led to Trump's success in these crucial swing states, but perhaps none more talked about than Hillary Clinton neglecting to campaign in Wisconsin.

Trump on the other hand was a force in Wisconsin, as well as Michigan, Ohio, Pennsylvania, and Florida. He held numerous rallies across the Midwest, barking into mics, going off script, and speaking off the cuff, even going so far as to encourage brawls in crowds at his rallies.

Regardless of what many think of his hate-mongering, he won. No doubt, we will be spending the next several decades debating the follies of the Democrats in 2016 as it was their election to lose.

Though analyzing what the Dems could have done differently is, of course, relevant and vital to their success in years to come, what I (and many others) have spent the past four years wondering is how *he* won.

Why did so many voters connect with him? What about the Trump brand was so alluring?

While politics has always been in part about a cult of personality, what stands out from Trump's rallies is the persona he projected, bolstered by his own personal narrative. Audiences felt an intimacy with Trump; his unfiltered nature convinced them the man on the podium was honest—the genuine article.

As voters, we want to understand who the person we vote for is. If it is human nature to fear what we do not understand, then it stands to reason we will fear presidential candidates we don't perceive as revealing of their personal side. While it has been proven much of what Trump spouted about himself, his wealth, and his family is categorically false, the stories he told forged a deep connection with their intended audience.

That's why it matters Trump is the person many want to grab a beer with. The feeling he inspires translates to votes, ultimately enabling him to garner enough of a response from the electorate to win.

Of course, Trump's base connected not only with his personal narrative, but with the anger and disenfranchisement he alluded to when speaking about his past. The documentary *#Unfit: The Psychology of Donald Trump* breaks down the psychology of the anger-based voting Trump inspired in 2016.[28]

In the film, former White House Communications Director Anthony Scaramucci notes, "[Trump] is a reflection of the cultural zeitgeist. He's an avatar of [our] anger. When he's lighting people up on Twitter, he's got a very large group of people in the United States actually giggling because they enjoy it."

---

28   "#Unfit: The Psychology of Donald Trump," directed by Dan Partland (2020), Doc Shop Productions, on Amazon Prime.

Where does that anger stem from? Racism, sexism, homophobia, xenophobia, and islamophobia, yes, but also years of feeling neglected during the Obama administration. Trump galvanized large swaths of white American voters after eight years of feeling their industries were ignored, their states diminished as "fly over" by coastal elites, and perhaps even more significantly, their worldview altered. A Black man was the most powerful person in the world, and that shook up the order of things as they knew it.

This view was cemented by Clinton's campaign. In 2016, speaking at a fundraising event in New York City, she was recorded saying you could put half of Trump supporters in a "basket of deplorables."[29]

If you're a rural voter who feels not only unheard, but also personally attacked and villainized by Clinton, Trump's personal attacks on the system become appealing. For many, a vote for Trump was inspired by anger as well as the sense of trust he builds with every tweet or off-the-cuff remark. He's able to voice so much without explicitly stating his opinion through his stories and comments. There is an implied deservedness in much of what he says—"of course I should have this"—with the implication that it's because he's a white, Christian man. The power of personal narrative to influence has much to do with what can go without being explicitly stated but is still communicated.

That feeling of connection is important. It is what drives us, and our decisions are largely influenced by the people whose stories and worldview reflect our own.

---

29 Katie Reilly, "Read Hillary Clinton's 'Basket of Deplorables' Remarks About Donald Trump Supporters," Time Magazine, September 10, 2016

When I worked for IBM, I had many managers. But two in particular explain why I believe interpersonal skills are so important to being a manager.

For the sake of anonymity, let's call her Alex. Alex was a 6'1" Israeli woman who commanded meetings with her thick-framed glasses and platform shoes. She spoke confidently and almost always had the best ideas in creative brainstorms. She was creative and inspirational and a ruthless critic and editor—everything that a young creative who sought to refine their craft wanted in a leader. But she did not open up often nor take much of an interest in her team's lives.

Now compare that with my next boss.

Alex quit abruptly to the sadness of her entire team, thinking no one could replace her. My next boss was different. Let's call him Chris. Chris was a short, quiet Canadian. A graphic designer by trade, he was a prominent executive creative director at media outlets like Fusion Media and legendary advertising agency Leo Burnett. Unlike Alex, Chris created space for others to speak up in meetings. He would often ask each of his team members, "Well, what do you think?" Chris also regularly scheduled after-work gatherings to make time to get to know each member of his team. We would get drinks, and he would tell us old war stories from the advertising world.

For a junior creative professional, someone like Alex was a dream to work for. I sat quietly and learned as much as I could from watching her process. Observing her develop campaign concepts (many of which went on to win industry awards) was a master class in marketing.

I worked harder for the person I felt like I knew better. I felt like Chris was real—maybe not a friend, per se, but someone who was willing to open up personally, which ultimately made me feel like he trusted me. That trust just made me feel more comfortable with him.

Through his efforts to forge personal relationships with his team, I also simply interacted with Chris more frequently. As a result, he—and, thus, the work I was doing for him—was more top of mind. I sensed he was invested in me in addition to my work. Eventually, I realized I enjoyed working for him and even enjoyed my individual work more. That personal connection I formed with Chris made a significant impact on me.

David Chang, popular chef and TV personality, has built an empire off connecting with people. His social media abounds with UGC focused on personal storytelling to customers and media. He's become an open book. Before the pandemic hit, his restaurants flourished and new locations sprouted up all across the country, from the flagship Momofuku Noodle Bar in New York's East Village to Momofuku Seiōbo in Sydney, Australia.

He is known for the innovative iconic dishes he's launched, like his pork buns (which started the American bun craze) and cereal milk soft serve (which has now become more popular via Christina Tosi's Milk Bar).

But his ability to scale his business cannot be entirely attributed to his acumen and creativity as a chef. He's a great marketer.

Chang realized early on people want to eat at restaurants that not only have excellent food, but also that they feel a personal connection to. He has been able to foster personal connections with customers around the world through social media by welcoming the world into his personal life.

As of this writing, his Instagram account has 1.6 million followers. Every week he posts photos and videos of the food he makes for his family. He discusses family drama, his views on current events, and even engages with his audience in the comments. "It was hot as fuck," he replied to one fan on Instagram.

He also openly connects with his own employees. "We are where we are in large part because of you..." he replied to a former employee on an Instagram post.

His social media accounts have turned into places to sincerely get to know the man behind the restaurant.

After viewing his Instagram stories, you feel you know Chang on a personal level. You want to eat ramen at one of his restaurants, regardless of your preference towards Japanese food, to support the man behind the concept.

I in no way mean to diminish the food Chang serves across his restaurant empire. The food is delicious, innovative, and the ultimate source of Chang's success. But he was able to scale from a cult phenomenon to a recognizable brand around the world by sharing his personal story through UGC.

The way in which UGC influences our emotions is not siloed in the restaurant world; it's also well established in pandemic-response politics.

New York governor Andrew Cuomo was a lesser-known politician prior to the spread of COVID-19. But during his daily briefings to the public, he became a star when there was no national leader stepping up.

The first and arguably hardest-hit state was New York. At the time I lived in the Upper West Side, and we felt the presence and pressures of the disease before the rest of the country. I remember my mom talking about freely going into grocery stores and indoor parties in California in March while New York City was just starting its strict lockdown.

Cuomo was thrown onto a worldwide stage as his state grappled with the spread of COVID-19. Meanwhile, his own president denied the seriousness of the disease in televised press conferences.

Cuomo didn't just step up to the challenge for his state; he filled the void left by the executive branch on the national stage. He was an early voice at the national level helping his fellow state governors prepare for what was to come.

As was one of first governors to hold daily press briefings, Cuomo had a ninety-six-day streak of press briefings lasting one hour or longer.

One *Vulture* headline even read, "Andrew Cuomo's Daily Press Briefing Is the Most Important Show on TV."[30]

---

30 Jen Chaney, "Andrew Cuomo's Daily Press Briefing Is the Most Important Show on TV," Vulture, March 26, 2020.

He sent a clear message to other governors: Our president will do nothing to prevent the spread of COVID-19, so it's up to us.

Cuomo's ratings shot up an astonishing thirty-two points during this time, giving him his best popularity ratings in seven years.[31]

The press briefings and media appearances were long, and Cuomo would regularly speak about his personal life. During an interview with CNN anchor Chris Cuomo, the governor's brother, he even playfully ribbed his younger sibling for being his mom's second-favorite son.

"I called mom just before I came on this show," Andrew Cuomo insisted. "By the way, she said I was her favorite. Good news is she said you are her second favorite. Second-favorite son, Christopher."[32]

The governor's ability to speak about his personal life during briefings and interviews built trust with the public.

We trust him because we know him. A quote from Professor Hitendra Wadhwa class may help us understand why.

"Personal stories make others feel like you are sharing 100 percent of yourself."

Stories build trust.

---

31 Mehta, Dhrumil, "Most Americans Like How Their Governor Is Handling The Coronavirus Outbreak," FiveThirtyEight, April 20, 2020.

32 Morgan Gstalter, "Cuomo brothers rib each other during CNN interview: 'There's always a time to call mom'," The Hill, March 2020.

According to the Open Society Foundations, there is a growing body of research in fields such as psychology, cognitive science, political science, and sociology demonstrating people do not make decisions through a purely rational process. Emotion and a range of cognitive biases play a hugely important role.

Personal storytelling has immense power. And the evolution of technology and media has made the growth of that power exponential. Twitter, Facebook, Instagram, and other platforms are allowing us to tell our stories in a real and sincere way.

CHAPTER 7

USER-GENERATED CONTENT & THE CITIZEN

People will vote for someone they don't like. They gave Richard Nixon a landslide. They don't like voting for people who don't like them.

ANTHONY SCARAMUCCI,
FORMER WHITE HOUSE COMMUNICATIONS DIRECTOR

I remember the moment President Obama won in 2008. I had just graduated from high school in Southern California, and we were watching the red and blue numbers tick up on CNN. It was just me and my mom in the living room, our eyes glued to the TV.

When they finally called the election and announced that Barack Obama would be the forty-fourth president of the United States, my mom began quietly crying.

"What's wrong? I thought you'd be happy he won," I asked her.

"I am. It's just different this time. Now someone with a name like ours is in the White House," she responded, standing next to the TV.

She meant someone with a funny name.

My mom's name is Latika (pronounced "Lah-tee-ka"). She regularly gets "Lee-tee-ka" or "Lay-tee-ka."

For a family of Indian Americans with nonwhite names, having a president named Barack *Hussein* Obama meant a lot. To us, it meant at some point in his life, our president had the experience of white people making fun of him. They asked him where he's *really* from. They called him a terrorist. They asked him why his mother would give him such a funny name. It meant he understood the feeling of alienation that follows those questions in a way no president before him likely had.

The 2016 election had a distinctly different feel. I was at the Red Derby, a bar in northwest Washington, DC, frequented by NGO and Capitol Hill staffers. At the beginning of the night the bar was crowded, hot and pulsing with anticipation of what we all assumed would be the election of the country's first female president. As we watched the returns come in, the mood of left-leaning millennials rose and fell like a bell curve. When they called the election in favor of Trump, we left devastated, many with tears in their eyes.

At the time my Republican friends told me not to be so dramatic. They were dubious but were willing to give Trump a chance. "You're being a typical East Coast liberal elite. He won fair and square. Give him a chance, and stop being so pessimistic." It only took a few months for them to realize Trump was no ordinary Republican leader, and his fascist authoritarian plans would damage both the country and their party.

No matter your political affiliation, if the years 2016–2020 gave you anxiety about the state of the country's liberal democratic system, you're not alone.

For many young people, the Clinton–Trump election of 2016 laid bare the social and political divide in our country on a scale never witnessed before. As a generation of digital natives, we were the first to broadcast our thoughts, ideas, and opinions to friends and family via social media.

For many months after that night at the Red Derby, I wondered what I could have done differently to bolster Hillary Clinton's campaign.

Could I have phone banked more, knocked on more doors, or donated more money? The answer is, of course, yes.

As the months continued, my thoughts turned from my commitment to her campaign toward my role as a citizen and voter.

Were my Republican friends right? Was I an elitist out of touch with the needs of my fellow citizens in other parts of the country?

Did I do enough to educate myself enough about Trump's platform and voters' needs? If I didn't do enough to support my candidate, what other mistakes have I made in my civic life? I started to ask myself how I fit inside this democracy.

In a world where we spend so much of our time on LinkedIn, Instagram, Facebook, Twitter, and other platforms, we often feel we're doing more than we actually are—liking and sharing a political thought piece, commenting on your favorite politician's recent post. We can be lulled into thinking our digital activism is as meaningful as activism in real life (IRL).

While we've never before had tools that empower the individual's voice to this degree, many of us struggle to bridge the gap between voicing our opinions online and contributing to real systemic change.

If our impetus to share our political perspectives online is an outgrowth of our desire to participate more fully in our democracy, what does the rise of UGC mean for our role as citizens in this country?

What does the intersection of digital and civic duty mean to us, the everyday individual citizens? How do we bring digital and civic spaces together to create the most impact?

As a recent college graduate, I considered myself a civically-minded individual. I registered to vote as soon as I turned eighteen, was active in political clubs, and even worked for government agencies such as the Department of Defense and the Department of Homeland Security.

As I started to make my own income, my focus started to shift from theoretical political debates to real-world responsibilities. I started to focus on my personal finances. I learned what a 401(k) is. What percentage of my take-home pay do I need to put into savings to survive? The time I put into political engagement quickly got put on the back burner as real life started to take shape. Your finances touch your life more immediately than politics. But I still always felt like I was an informed citizen.

In *The Good Citizen*, author Michael Schudson puts the role and the very concept of citizenry in historical context.[33] He posits five different eras of citizenship in America since the eighteenth century. In each of these eras, to be a "citizen" meant something entirely different.

During the first era, roughly the late eighteenth to the early-nineteenth century, engaged citizenship was defined by the politics of assent. Of course, citizenship was also limited to a very small portion of the populous, primarily white landowning men. On election day, a citizen would stand at a podium and publicly shout the name of the nominee he voted for. After voting he would be handed a jug of ale by the party member he endorsed and slapped on the back by fellow supporters.

In the second era following the turn of the nineteenth to late-nineteenth century came the rise of party politics. During this period, citizenship was still limited to adult white males, but the right to vote no longer required property ownership. This was a significant change in the history of American voting. The citizen was no longer one of assent but rather tied to a political party. This period was marked

---

33 Michael Schudson, The Good Citizen, (Reprint Edition, New York: Free Press, 2011) 188-189.

by party loyalty and rituals of solidarity for your side. Think lavish parties, tall hats, and ornate banners celebrating your party's candidate.

The third era Schudson defines is the "informed citizen." This era heralded many changes for the individual voter. The Australian secret ballot was introduced, and voting shifted from a public display of loyalty to your party to a private civic duty for the individual. Campaigning near polling stations was forbidden. Gifts that parties could give to voters were strictly limited. Those who advocated for these reforms endeavored to transform political campaigning from an act based on emotions to one grounded in education. If you've tuned into Fox News lately, I think you can see we are reverting to emotional debates instead of ones based on facts.

The civil rights movement defined the fourth era. Schudson calls it the time of the "rights-bearing citizen," who succeeded in broadening the space of politics. The polling station was no longer the center of civic participation but one of many locations where citizenship could be exercised and enacted. Being a citizen was no longer defined by the act of voting alone. Homes, classrooms, courtrooms, and interest groups all became equal repositories for political activity.

The book made me realize the time we are in today—the age of Trump and nefarious storytellers most resembles this second era. Our connection to party rhetoric and holding the party line is similar to how voters engaged with politics in the 1890s.

Mainstream media has played a crucial role in the growth of partisan politics. The resurgence of the kind of divisive party politics that existed in the nineteenth century is in large part stoked by the marketing of network giants like Fox News. Fox, well aware that nuanced fact- and evidence-based reporting does not rate as highly as opinion-based reporting in the age of social media, has doubled down on its emotionally evocative journalism focus. As CEO of Fox News Roger Ailes said in 1998, "If you come out and try to do right-wing news, you're going to die. You can't get away with it."

As Reece Peck writes in *Fox Populism*, "[The] potent mix of tabloid taste and populist moral reasoning is the crux of how Fox News has interpellated its audience as the 'authentic,' working-class majority, thus allowing it to effectively re-present narrow conservative political demands as popular and universal."[34]

Fox News capitalizes off the division it sows. We may not be drinking champagne in the streets to celebrate our candidates but entertainment-style politics is just as big now as it was in the nineteenth century. Ailes (now deceased) was well aware conservative viewers were too preoccupied by the elements of their lives that demanded immediate attention (personal finances, job security, health care) to care about the details of political news. He knew their outlets would have to evoke an emotional response to resonate with audiences. This is seen in Fox News' advertising every day.

A 2009 promo for Bill O'Reilly's show, *The O'Reilly Factor*, is a good example.

---

34   Reece Peck, Fox Populism. New York: Cambridge University Press, 2019.

In capital letters, an ad for the show reads: "THE ULTIMATE IN CONFRONTATION TV. A REAL VOICE FOR THE LITTLE GUY. LOVE HIM. HATE HIM. HE'S CLEARLY NUMBER ONE."

Fox News' marketing team takes its cues from reality TV ads.

As more viewers cut cable, populist style news personalities build their brand platforms through UGC online.

Take nefarious storyteller and conservative commentator Ben Shapiro for example. He has over 982,000 subscribers on his Snapchat program, *The Ben Shapiro Show*, and one of the most listened to podcasts on Apple Podcasts. He was able to transition seamlessly from the now defunct Breitbart News Network.

Hopefully, coming to terms with the fact that media outlets capitalize on the growth of personal and moralistic content on cable and social media will make *all* viewers be more discerning when watching emotionally intense political narratives.

Schudson concludes with the argument that good citizens do not necessarily need to be fully informed, to have political beliefs. People cannot possibly be fully informed due to the mere fact that there is simply too much information available to us. None of the four models of citizenship would meet the demands of the average citizen in our present-day environment.

The rise of party politics and the rise of the information age create an interesting juxtaposition.

Today, there is simply too much information for the everyday citizen to be fully politically informed. For example, the state voter guide for California is 126 pages long, full of incredibly dense prose.[35] Every registered voter receives a copy in the mail and is expected to read it. If you've ever actually read a voter guide, you've encountered technical language, often intentionally confusing verbiage, and legalese that is difficult to decipher. Even fully understanding each of your representatives' platforms, from local up to presidential, on a ballot can be a challenge.

That's where our political parties' tags come into play.

Party labels help citizens wade through the slog of too much information and quickly identify initiatives they will support. Party labels provide the illusion of making an informed choice. As Schudson argues, we use party labels as a cue—a source of quick information on whether we agree or disagree. This has led to the phenomenon of down-ballot voting, or voting along party lines. We're in an age of infinite access to information, and we are overwhelmed.

UGC and what it means to be a good citizen go hand in hand. The evolution of the responsibilities of the individual citizen is core to Schudson's book. And I believe an individual's digital narrative presence is a new concept that should be added to those civic responsibilities. We should all aspire to be socially conscious storytellers through our UGC online. If the book were to be updated for today, Schudson may argue our social media profiles are deeply intertwined with our roles as citizens.

---

35   Michael Schudson, "The Good Citizen," C-Span, November 6, 1998.

Our biggest responsibility as digital citizens is to be vigilant consumers of information online.

As barriers to disseminate information decrease, we must become more conscious consumers. Nefarious storytellers abound and gain more credibility with every like and share, no matter their proximity to the truth. Of course, we need to be mindful of what we read and watch online. But what's more, we need to be aware of our emotional responses when encountering personal narratives online. We must be perhaps our most vigilant when connecting with a story, because our desire to experience that connection can often supplant our instinct to investigate whether it is real or based in fact.

If we lead our digital gaze away from misleading stories, we may be able to remove from office politicians who exploit our deepest fears and move away from our current time of hard-line party politics.

As we become more critical consumers of UGC in our digital civic spaces on Facebook and Twitter, we can make space and room for political leaders who represent both passion and rationality.

CHAPTER 8

EMPOWERING THE SOCIALLY CONSCIOUS STORYTELLER

───

There's a lot I still don't know about America, about life, about what the future might bring. But I do know myself. My father, Fraser, taught me to work hard, laugh often, and keep my word. My mother, Marian, showed me how to think for myself and to use my voice. Together, in our cramped apartment on the South Side of Chicago, they helped me see the value in our story, in my story, in the larger story of our country. Even when it's more real than you want it to be. Your story is what you have, what you will always have. It is something you own.

MICHELLE OBAMA, BECOMING

Walter McMillian, a Black man from the South, was forty-seven when sent to prison for the wrongful accusation of murdering eighteen-year-old Ronda Morrison, a white woman, in 1986. The night the young girl was murdered in Monroeville, Alabama, McMillian was far from the scene of the crime at a family picnic with numerous witnesses—one of them even a cop.

On June 17, 1987, he was sent to the Holman Correctional Facility in Atmore, Alabama, by the bigoted sheriff Tom Tate. There he spent fifteen months waiting for his first trial. Luckily for McMillian, up-and-coming activist lawyer and Harvard Law graduate Bryan Stevenson took his case. After spending six years on death row for the conviction of a crime he did not commit, he was released from prison.

In large part due to my racial and class identities, I've never had any significant encounters with law enforcement. So, it took reading McMillian's story in the novel *Just Mercy* to understand the deep injustice inherent in the American penal system. His story humanized the numbers behind the statistics that illustrate the scale of mass incarceration in the United States. McMillian's journey through the criminal justice system reveals the discriminatory, tedious, and racist practices within it.

McMillian was ultimately cleared, did not have to face the electric chair, and was able to reunite with his family. Unfortunately, that is not a guaranteed outcome for many Black men incarcerated in the US penal system.[36]

---

36 Bryan Stevenson, Just Mercy, (Trade Paperback Edition, New York: Random House, 2015) 67.

Here are a few statistics that help put the problem of mass incarceration in the United States in perspective:[37]

- The prison population in the United States has increased from 300,000 in the early 1970s to 2.3 million in 2014.

- One in every three Black male babies born this century is expected to be incarcerated.

- About 65 percent of people in jail have not yet been convicted of a crime; they just can't pay bail.

Even more jaw-dropping is the fact that significant criminal justice reform at a national level has never really happened.

In 2020 I, like so many other people around the world, was shaken by videos capturing graphic killings of Black men in the United States. As a person of color, I've always been aware of issues surrounding race, but watching numerous Black citizens dehumanized, antagonized, bullied, othered, and murdered on camera changed everything for me.

In 2020, we saw a spike in media attention on the issues of mass incarceration and the over-policing of Black and brown communities in America. As more murders of citizens by police were caught on camera, the country stood witness.

From the chilling footage of police suffocating Eric Garner to death in Staten Island, New York, to the murder of

---

37 Daniele Selby, "The Surprising Mission Behind Conbody'S 'Prison-Style' Workouts," Global Citizen, May 15, 2019.

George Floyd in Minneapolis, Minnesota, it felt like many non-Black Americans started to see institutionalized racism play out before our eyes overnight. What we are witnessing in the United States is the slaughter and mass incarceration of innocent Black men due to the unconscious bias and outright racism of a system meant to protect the citizenry and a police force emboldened by an openly bigoted administration.

I remember the moment I saw the viral video of five police officers violently pinning Garner to the ground. As I sat in my bedroom in Washington, DC, I could feel myself becoming physically ill as the cops slowly surrounded Garner. It felt like wolves intimidating their prey. When they jumped on Garner's back, tears streamed down my face, and I yelled out, "No, no, no, stop!" Like so many others who bore witness to this violent abuse of power and disregard for Garner's life, I found myself shouting at my phone, staring in disbelief, and feeling completely overwhelmed with sadness. No one has the right to take another person's life, never mind the fact that Garner was not guilty of any crime. Police were attracted to the area because Garner broke up a fight between two other people. He died because he was trying to do something good.

Many people have written about the proliferation of videos capturing violence against Black people in America as a driving force behind police reform efforts, broader conversations about race in America, and the Black Lives Matter movement. The video capturing the inhumane treatment of Eric Garner opened my eyes to the ways in which racism is deeply ingrained in policing and the constant vigilance Black men must adopt to survive in America. I wish it didn't take a fellow human losing their life to help me realize this.

There's an argument to be made about the problems of virality and violence porn. To some, sharing these kinds of videos is seen as insensitive, while for others, having to face these videos when they pull up their social media accounts is deeply painful and traumatizing. This discussion is deeply important and, in some cases, has led to a more thoughtful treatment of these videos by media outlets, influencers, and citizens. But there is no question that the cameras on our phones are indispensable tools in the fight for change. Individual citizens are now able to shed a spotlight on the injustices Black men and women have had to contend with in America for centuries.

Whether it's the momentum of the Black Lives Matter movement, the fourth year of the Trump presidency, or the COVID-19 pandemic, many young Americans are feeling called to action. The common human experience right now is one of distress and anxiety. But our common obstacles bond us together. We are being moved to action, and we want our voices heard. We want to act. And thanks to the new media technology sphere, we have an opportunity to make positive use of our UGC to spread awareness, educate, and advocate against injustice.

During my last year in business school, I participated in a course that connects MBAs with formerly incarcerated people (FIPs). In the ReEntry Acceleration Program (REAP), my peers and I were able to speak with former inmates about their experience returning to society from correctional centers. The obstacles they faced were numerous, and the lack of programs to help FIPs reacclimate to society shocked me.

FIPs deal with the overwhelming number of choices one must make every day. From navigating public transportation to simply choosing what clothes to wear, FIPs return to a world that may look quite different than the one they knew prior to their incarceration, without the tools or support needed to ensure they succeed.

Being released from prison is a process mired in complications. The circumstance can vary from state to state, but it is not uncommon for FIPs who have spent fifteen or more years in a correctional facility to be released with nothing more than a few bus tickets, $50, and the clothes from their time in prison. Many are also stripped of their voting rights. According to the legal services–focused nonprofit Equal Justice Initiative, past criminal convictions prevent approximately six million Americans from voting.[38] Added to that are the responsibilities they are saddled with upon release: meetings with case managers, finding housing, and obtaining a job.

In REAP, we heard from FIPs who started successful entrepreneurial enterprises despite these reentry obstacles. Meeting the mass incarceration problem face-to-face for the first time, I realized a place those of us privileged enough never to interact with the criminal justice system can put our energy: listening, following, and sharing stories from FIPs on social media and supporting programs that specifically support FIPs through reentry.

In many states, there is often an unofficial pipeline between correctional facilities and homeless shelters. When FIPs are

---

38 EJI Staff, "Support Grows For Restoration Of Voting Rights To Formerly Incarcerated People In Alabama," Equal Justice Initiative, February 1, 2016.

released, many don't have a home to go back to, not just because they've lost contact with family and friends, but also because many connections have passed away during the many years they've spent in correctional facilities. So they go straight to facilities with free housing. And shelters are often hotbeds full of crime and drugs.

"It's like we're cattle. You go from one holding area to another holding area. But at least here, you got the opportunity to get out there and do something to try and make it," says Christopher Kaminski, an FIP who spoke with NY1 News.[39]

Kaminski has been in and out of prisons for more than twenty-six years. After his release in 2018, he was sent straight to Bellevue Men's Shelter on the East Side of Manhattan. A week after his release he succumbed to purchasing a six-dollar bag of heroin in another shelter.

"As soon as he said, I have a bag for six dollars, anybody interested? I said, you know what? I haven't done one in ten years. F---in stressed out, bored to death, hating this place, let me get this bag, and maybe it will ease some of the stress. It didn't do nothing. It just made things worse," Kaminski said.

Kaminski is not alone. Nonprofits like the American Civil Liberties Union and Southern Poverty Law Center often speak about the challenges facing FIPs returning to society.

---

39   Courtney Gross, "NEW YORK'S PRISON PIPELINE," Metrofocus/NY1, March 15, 2018.

Rarely though do we hear from the FIPs themselves.

Journalists and media outlets have historically been the storytellers of society. They are gatekeepers of current events and news and for good reason. They play a critical role in speaking truth to power and holding those in leadership positions accountable for the decisions they make.

But the role of the institutional publisher is fundamentally changing. Younger audiences aren't following CNN or Fox News on their social media channels, instead gravitating toward individuals like Tucker Carlson and Anderson Cooper. We want to see and hear from people, not brands. The digital revolution and the expanding role of social media have had an incredible ripple effect on tech-media norms. The shift in consumer focus from institutional brands to personal narratives is all around us, in politics, business, entertainment, and sports. There's a newfound appreciation for the individual to own their story and even turn themselves into a business. And within that lies an opportunity for FIPs to become socially conscious storytellers and tell more stories through UGC.

Thanks in large part to smartphone technology and creative storytelling software (Figma, Instagram, Sketch, Adobe, Squarespace, and Canva, to name a few), the socially conscious storyteller is empowered like never before to tell their story online, reaching audiences on their own. Many returning FIPs have missed the digital revolution. The content-driven world is drastically different than the cable-driven one many of them left. As returning citizens, those that have the desire to share their story have an opportunity to do so with the full arsenal of tools from the digital boom. They have the power to write their narrative and educate in the process of telling their stories.

The video storytelling process has drastically evolved over the past few years. No longer do you need to hire an expensive video editor or buy fancy cameras to create compelling videos. All you need is a camera-enabled phone.

From Instagram to LinkedIn, numerous platforms allow individual creators to build—and more importantly, own—their narratives. For FIPs, the proliferation of social media platforms coupled with access to high-quality storytelling tools can increase the success of their reentry process by supplementing a traditional CV and helping them to secure a job or housing.

Coss Marte, a New York–based fitness entrepreneur, has leveraged these tools and platforms to tell his story.

Marte was born and raised in New York City. In 2005, he was sent to prison for running a multimillion-dollar cocaine operation. He spent ten years in and out of Riker's Island, New York's notorious prison complex, due to his drug-related crimes. In the midst of his jail time, Marte faced severe health issues.

He was overweight, and doctors warned him if he continued with his current lifestyle, he would likely die young from health-related issues.

"He was overweight when he was locked up—at 5 feet, 8 inches tall, he weighed over 230 pounds. Prison doctors, he says, gave him a grim prognosis—he might not live to be released," writes George Bodarky in a story profiling Marte for NPR.[40]

During his time on the "inside," he realized he needed to stay out of trouble and become healthier. He discovered a passion for fitness and lost a staggering seventy pounds in six months by creating body weight–focused workouts in his nine-by-six-foot jail cell. He didn't have much space but made use of every square inch, doing jumping jacks, squats, and planks. These workouts would end up being critical to Marte's future non-drug-related business.

Marte transitioned his custom workouts into products and launched a prison boot camp–style fitness startup called CONBODY: workouts that are meant for tiny spaces, with no equipment.

According to the CONBODY website, "CONBODY is a prison style fitness bootcamp that hires formerly incarcerated individuals to teach fitness classes. CONBODY…is the ultimate no-equipment, workout program." Marte utilized his story to take on an entrepreneurial enterprise that taught clients how to work out anyplace, anytime.

In an interview with famed internet media entrepreneur Gary Vaynerchuk, Marte talked about his upbringing and story in detail: "I grew up in a neighborhood that was very drug infested in the 80s and 90s…my mom emigrated from the Dominican Republic when she was six months pregnant

---

40   George Bodarky, "From Jail Cell To Studio: Drug Dealer Becomes Personal Trainer," National Public Radio, January 2, 2015.

with me; she ended up working in a factory. She babysat me under her sewing machine, and that's how I lived."[41]

Growing up in Manhattan's Lower East Side, Marte was surrounded by drugs.

"I saw the guys that were on my corner who, you know, wore the chains…had the girls, the cars, and I saw that they were making money. There was a lot. It was crazy how there was heroin lines down the block…people buying drugs off of them. I saw that as an avenue to becoming rich."

Marte started selling at thirteen. By the time he was nineteen, he was making over two million dollars a year.

"You know back in the day I saw individuals standing on the corner [selling] drugs. I made a whole delivery service."

Marte didn't just sell drugs: he brought numerous innovations to the old way of selling drugs. Instead of following what others were doing, he brought the product directly to the consumer through on-demand delivery (a novel idea at the time). Members of his team wore suits, found clients in upscale Wall Street restaurants, and even had business cards. He turned the drug world on its head and revolutionized an industry.

Marte asserts it wasn't a love for drugs that made him successful but his passion for business. He took that same entrepreneurial spirit to CONBODY.

---

41   Gary Vee, "CONBODY's Coss Marte chats with #GaryVee on #MarketingForTheNow episode #8!" YouTube Video, 16:01, August 3, 2020.

Rather than relying on traditional forms of advertising (paper ads, TV spots, flyers) Marte crafted his story for a digital audience.

He created an Instagram account, started a podcast, and wrote a book. He spent time teaching himself about new media and utilized free online tools to strengthen his story, which ultimately went viral.

His followers and audiences on social media platforms converted into paying customers. Now, CONBODY's customers are numbered in the thousands and Marte has even opened a physical location in the same neighborhood where he used to sell drugs—Manhattan's Lower East Side. Marte was able to capitalize on his past experiences by harnessing the power of his personal story—a significant example of what is possible when someone is given the right storytelling tools. This is the premise on which I built my venture, Terra Digital.

In 2020, I launched Terra to help socially conscious storytellers like Marte. If he could capitalize on his story and find success, why couldn't others? Terra Digital is a video platform for content creators without any video editing expertise. Our mission is to empower socially conscious storytellers to tell their stories more effectively in the digital space. In a world full of digital video content, creating a video with a compelling story is still complex and expensive. Most creators don't have $5,000 to spend on a freelance video editor or director in Brooklyn. They have to do it themselves. But we aim to help.

By crafting premium storyboarded templates and automated computer vision software, we transform your user-generated content (i.e., the videos on your phone) into editorially driven stories with strong narrative arcs. Terra is a video platform aimed at solving one simple problem: making video storytelling easier and more accessible.

Prior to bearing witness to Eric Garner's death, I read reports and digested data that prove there is a deeply-rooted problem with mass incarceration in this country. I'm loath to admit it, but I became inured to the data. I all but expected to see inequity in the numbers. What has had a far more lasting effect on me are the stories of those affected by our criminal justice system: Eric Garner's death at the hands of law enforcement and Coss Marte's story. These are the things that have not only made an indelible impression but have also influenced the way I and many others choose to invest in our communities and agitate for change.

What if we were able to give more people the tools to tell their story like Coss Marte? What if every individual affected by climate change or fighting for immigration reform had the chance to tell their story?

If we give every citizen the tools to tell their own story, we may be able to inspire true systemic change—not by relying solely on data to justify a position, but by winning the hearts and minds of policymakers through real human storytelling. If we can do that, maybe we can convince those in power in Washington, DC, to enact substantial reform.

CHAPTER 9

PERSONAL NARRATIVE STORYTELLING, CONSPIRACY THEORIES, AND THE DARK SIDE OF THE DIGITAL BOOM

President Trump has proven time and time again he is no friend of the historically disenfranchised.

On May 1, 1989, Trump took out four full-page ads in New York City newspapers, including in the *New York Times*, that read, "BRING BACK THE DEATH PENALTY. BRING BACK OUR POLICE!" in all capital letters.

The copy was crafted to rouse pressure to prosecute the Central Park Five: a group of young Black and Latino teenagers wrongfully convicted of raping twenty-eight-year-old Trisha Meili.

"I want to hate these murderers and I always will. I am not looking to psychoanalyze or understand them, I am looking to punish them," Trump wrote in the ad.[42]

The wrongful sentencing of the Central Park Five is now one of the most infamous American injustices in US history.

On the night of April 19, 1989, Meili was jogging in Central Park when she was brutally beaten and raped. Eager to make arrests in the case, police rounded up Kevin Richardson, Antron McCray, Raymond Santana, Korey Wise, and Yusef Salaam, five young boys who happened to be in the park at the same time of the attack, coercing them into pleading guilty. All five subsequently spent years in prison for a crime they did not commit. Only in 2002 did serial rapist Matias Reyes confess to the attack on Meili, exonerating the young men.

Numerous books, news articles, and even a Netflix series called *When They See Us* describe how the criminal justice system actively worked against the boys and their families. Lawyers and police officers convinced the boys to plead guilty to appease growing public pressure. Trump helped inflame the public's focus (and panic) with his advertisement, while officials looked to reinstall public trust in government and the police force by finding the culprits quickly.

When asked by a reporter in 2019 if he'd apologize for the egregious mistake, Trump responded, "You have people on

---

42 Jan Ransom, "Trump Will Not Apologize for Calling for Death Penalty Over Central Park Five," The New York Times, June 18, 2019.

both sides of that...they admitted their guilt." He not only refused to apologize but also denied the innocence of the five men.

Trump no longer has to take out ads in local newspapers to distort what is true and what is false. He can rouse the public from a far larger platform now on social media.

Trump and his loyalists have always read from the same script but now they have a bigger audience. It's not only the content of his speeches or tweets that led to Trump's ascendance to the presidency, but also the number of viewers he consistently reaches.

His audience on social media isn't just made of staunch supporters. His posts are for those of us obsessed with the drama.

A friend from graduate school, who describes himself as a "die-hard liberal," recently showed me an Instagram post. It was a meme of President Trump.

The words "Trump Suggests Injecting Disinfectant Shining UV Light Inside Patients to Kill Coronavirus in Bizarre, Rambling Tangent" sat above a photo of the President making a goofy smile.

"Can you believe that?" he asked, after I read it.

"Believe what?" I said, assuming it was a joke.

"That he said that?!"

"Well, that's from a meme Instagram account. I think it's just a joke, like *The Onion*. I don't think we can assume it's a fact that he said those words."

"No. He said it, I know it," he said, confidently looking at the thousands of likes and comments on the post.

The post was by a meme account dedicated to creating political satire around the administration. While we later learned Trump did in fact suggest injecting disinfectant into your body could cure the virus, my friend believed what she read on Instagram well before confirming its verification by a credible news source.

In *The Drama of Celebrity,* Sharon Marcus helps explain why we are captive to outrageous antics, even when they come out of the White House during a national crisis.

"Donald Trump was already a reality TV star when he ran for president in 2016. Early in his campaign, he attracted millions of outraged critics after he slurred Mexicans, mocked a disabled reporter, and boasted about committing sexual assaults. But Trump also garnered millions of admirers, and reporters had no trouble finding many Americans willing to go on the record hailing him as an unapologetic maverick willing to defy political correctness. For better and for worse, celebrities have long attracted interest and even adoration for being unruly."[43]

Defiance, Marcus argues, is the crux of why we care.

---

43 Sharon Marcus, The Drama of Celebrity, (New York: Princeton University Press, 2019) 200.

"Celebrities, by boldly making their shows of defiance public, do more than simply display unconventionality. They model an emotional attitude of indifference to nonconformity's potential consequences."

What is the consequence of this obsession with defiance? Well, a distorted reality.

The news is a bizarre place right now. In the time of President Trump, we tend to believe what we read, or at least question what we know to be true. And that is, in fact, the goal of nefarious storytellers like Trump.

It's not just the unprecedented political times that render us gullible. Our obsession with reality TV stars is intrinsically linked to the rise of social media and the subsequent rise of the individual content creator.

Nefarious storytellers exploit our desire to connect through stories and leverage the trust they've built with their audience to promote their own version of reality. They draw on our compulsion to believe those we feel closer to emotionally and to pull us away from those with fact-based perspectives: academics, scientists, or journalists. We operate on instinct and validation from our "social connections," not dry statistics or reports.

While the digital revolution has led to new opportunities for socially conscious storytellers like Coss Marte, it has also had a dark, reality-bending effect on collective psyche, as propelled by nefarious storytellers.

Personal narrative storytelling makes us feel like we are having a conversation with someone who understands us fully. Without an actual exchange, we can feel seen and heard because someone else's experience or worldview reflects our own.

It has the power to make us believe our most inner thoughts. We can now manufacture validity for thoughts that may not be based in reality.

Her, a 2013 American science fiction movie starring Joaquin Phoenix, was released just six years after the first iPhone was launched. In it, Theodore, Phoenix's character, falls in love with a robot on his smartphone powered by artificial intelligence. Samantha, the AI conversation application, develops and learns based on the conversation "she" has with her user.

Eventually, Theodore, an admittedly emotionally vulnerable protagonist, becomes so infatuated with the robot he loses his grasp on reality. He fades away from friends and family, spending all his time with his new digital companion.

What Theodore doesn't fully comprehend is that he has been feeding himself his own ideas, thoughts, and emotions through the application. He does not (nor does he want to) realize Samantha is a reflection of himself—an entity solely based on his actions.

He stops seeing the seemingly obvious when he starts feeling comforted by Samantha's remarks. She helps distract Theodore from the real world. By creating a new reality with Samantha, he can ignore and ultimately suppress his insecurities about his love life. This new reality makes Theodore forget about his very real depression and the loss of his wife.

Through Samantha, filmmaker Spike Jonze provides a very apt metaphor for the lives we live on our mobile devices today. A version of Samantha is very much alive in all our social media feeds.

We are empowered to pick and choose who we follow on Twitter, Facebook, and Instagram. While we get to customize the kind of content we see and hear, the algorithm behind these platforms feed us more and more content based on those preferences—much like how Samantha evolves with Theodore's interactions or the Trump memes social media feeds serve my friend.

Now more than ever, we are able to customize what we consume. If we are naturally inclined to trust the accounts we follow, these accounts begin to influence what we see as fact or fiction based. Our reality is shaped by the content of our feeds.

The self-perpetuating cycle Theodore experienced with Samantha is the same we find ourselves in when scrolling through our social media accounts in the morning or before we go to bed. We live in self-selecting realities. Every time we engage with our feeds, we become more and more myopic. The space we allow for alternate perspectives or dissenting information is shrinking.

Though *Her* was met with mixed reviews, it holds a mirror up to our relationship with social media and the problems it poses to society. The deep personalization of what is, for many, our primary source of news and opinion, has had massive psychological effects on the way we decipher and decode reality. It's also had very real implications for the world of politics.

The version of reality we create for ourselves in our digital bubbles has led to a distinct rise in populist rhetoric in US politics.

It would be an understatement to say there is a deep political divide in the United States. Understanding how our interactions with digital media have aided this divide may help repair it.

In *What Is Populism?* Jan-Werner Müller attempts to break down and define the characteristics of populism. He notes a few common themes:

1. Populism is a particular moralistic imagination of politics, a way of perceiving the political world that sets a morally pure and fully unified people against elites who are corrupt and morally flawed.

2. Populists claim to represent "the people" or "the will of the people" or "the real America" or "the silent majority." A vague and general populace.

3. Populists are inherently anti-pluralist and claim opponents are illegitimate.

He posits many more characteristics, but these stand out as significant in our current political environment. The 2016 presidential election saw many of the above themes play out in both campaigns. Candidates Clinton and Trump used various digital media communication tactics to delegitimize the other and gain trust from voters.

During his 2016 presidential campaign (and well before), Donald Trump fueled rumors about President Barack Obama's true origin of birth. He used this rumor as positive proof of the narrative he built—that hardworking, white, blue-collar people were the true Americans while nonwhites and a corrupt elite were interlopers trying to take the country from them.

"The controversy over Barack Obama's birth certificate made this logic almost ridiculously obvious and literal: at the same time, the president managed to embody in the eyes of the right-wingers both the 'bicoastal elite' and the African American Other; neither of which belongs to the United Stated proper."[44]

Through this personal attack questioning Obama's birthplace and eligibility, Trump was able to communicate his belief about just who America belongs to, confirming the beliefs of his followers. He was able to steer the conversation away from substantive policy discussions towards delegitimizing Obama altogether. The divide the "birther movement" created allowed him to grow his base. A substantial number of Americans believed Trump.

Of course, his claims are categorically false. Obama was born in Honolulu, Hawaii, and released his birth certificate that

---

44   Jan-Werner Muller, What is Populism? (University of Pennsylvania Press, 2016) 77.

documents this fact in 2008. Nonetheless, people continued to believe the false claims. According to a 2016 Morning Consult poll, only 62 percent of Americans believed Obama was born in the United States.[45]

While there has been much discussion around the myriad reasons why voters would choose to believe this falsehood, there is no denying many were convinced by Trump. They trusted Trump. He spent his career as a reality TV star and his campaign claiming to be an open book. He purported to let the American voter inside his head. Certainly, his gaffs could allow one to feel that we saw exactly what he was thinking at all times. That raw sincerity, as bombastic as it was, made him beloved. His followers took what he said at face value, despite the fact-based reporting from credible news outlets that proved his claims were often false. In many ways, they had a difficult time keeping up. Why read the boring news, when you could listen to Trump saying something wild and brand new?

His Twitter account was a critical tool in his ability to engage in "direct" communication. His social media channels were alluring platforms for Americans who wanted to get to know him—here was an arena in which to connect with the "real" Trump.

"Real Americans can be done with the media and have direct access (or, rather, the illusion of direct contact with) a man who is not just a celebrity; the self-described 'Hemingway of 140 characters' uniquely tells it like it is," Muller writes.

---

45   Kyle Dropp and Brendan Nyhan, "It Lives. Birtherism Is Diminished but Far From Dead," The New York Times, September 23, 2016.

Muller refers to this access as "direct representation."

"Everything that might contradict what we are already thinking is silenced in the echo chamber of the internet. The web (and a leader like Trump) always have an answer—and, amazingly, it always happens to be the one we were expecting."

The echo chambers of social media feeds leave little room for moderating influences. There are no pundits to make us question our gut reactions and no intermediaries—just direct, unfiltered access to people who already share or reinforce our perspective.

While there's no denying the current tech-media sphere has greatly benefited society, it would be foolish not to acknowledge the ways in which it can divide and harm. Nefarious storytellers have the same access to media tools and can spread stories with a different goal in mind: dismantling reality to benefit themselves.

Social media has created a myopic digital world. And that in turn has influenced the rise in conspiracy theories. Trump is well aware of this. His populist style of leadership has made him an infallible actor in the eyes of his supporters. To many, Trump can do no wrong, so any failures under his leadership must have an alternate source.

"The problem is never the populist's imperfect capacity to represent the people's will; rather, it's always the institutions that somehow produce the wrong outcomes. So even if they look properly democratic, there must be something going on behind the scenes that allow corrupt elites to continue to betray the people. Conspiracy theories are thus not a curious addition to populist rhetoric; they are rooted in and emerge from the very logic of populism itself," Muller argues.

The infamous Pizzagate scandal is yet another example of how Trump was able to make us question what is real and what is not.

In November 2016, the email account of John Podesta, Clinton's campaign manager, was hacked and his emails released by Wikileaks. One of the emails is between Podesta and the owner of the Washington, DC, restaurant Comet Ping Pong.

A completely random user on a far-right conspiracy website comment board known as 4chan (a predecessor to QAnon) began speculating the pizzeria was the headquarters of a child trafficking ring led by Clinton and Podesta. The rumor snowballed across white supremacist message boards. Some shared it as a joke about a hated figure, but others sincerely believed it to be true. Hundreds of individuals sat behind their keyboards and gave life to the baseless claim. The conspiracy culminated with a man so disturbed by the rumor he went to the restaurant armed with a gun thinking he would save the children.

On December 4, 2016, twenty-eight-year-old Edgar Maddison Welch walked into Comet Ping Pong and pointed an assault rifle in the direction of waiters and staff. He fired off shots inside the restaurant while looking for the child sex trafficking ring. No one was hurt, and Welch was arrested when he realized he was wrong.[46]

---

46   Michael Sebastion and Gabrielle Bruney, "What is Pizzagate?" Esquire, July 24, 2020.

The birther conspiracy and Pizzagate are grim and depressing reminders of the consequences of digital storytelling and UGC generated in silos.

It's an interesting conundrum we find ourselves in. The digital revolution has led to countless ways to communicate, tell stories, and access information. But what has that unbridled access to the world led to? Has it helped us better understand what's around us, or has it blurred the lines of reality?

In their new book *A Lot of People Are Saying*, Russel Muirhead and Nancy L. Rosenblum argue there is a new kind of assault on reality. The digital boom has led to a frightening evolution of conspiracy theories via "new conspiracism" that seeks to replace evidence, argument, and shared grounds of understanding with convoluted conjurings and bare assertions.

What validates conspiracies in the twenty-first century is not evidence, but repetition.

"When Trump tweeted the accusation that President Barack Obama had ordered the FBI to tap his phones in October before the 2016 election, no evidence of the charge was forthcoming. What mattered was not evidence but the number of retweets the president's post would enjoy: the more retweets, the more credible the charge," Muirhead and Rosenblum write.[47]

"...these are how doubts are instilled and accusations are validated in the new media. The new conspiracism—all

---

47 Russel Muirhead and Nancy L. Rosenblum, A Lot of People Are Saying, (Princeton University Press. Preface to paperback edition: Princeton, New Jersey. 2019) 98.

accusation, no evidence—substitutes social validation for scientific validation: if a lot of people are saying it…then it is true enough."

Our curated feeds deliver us this social validation. Our feeds confirm our gut feelings.

This is a consequence of the massive amount of information we consume today. What happens when we are bombarded with so much information that it becomes exhausting and overwhelming? We don't go through the laborious task of fact-checking, so we trust the only truth that matters—our own.

4chan is far from the only conspiracy movement Trump has latched onto to spread misinformation. The recent rise of QAnon has gained terrifying speed and is regularly lauded by President Trump.

Reply All, a podcast featuring "stories about how people shape the internet, and how the internet shapes people" from Gimlet Media, provides critical historical context to the evolution of QAnon. In episode 166 called "Country of Liars," the hosts, PJ Vogt and Alex Goldman, take on the daunting task of explaining what QAnon is and how it relates to the president—no small task for an opaque organization that prides itself on secrecy.[48]

The investigation takes the hosts back to the beginning of the QAnon scam and to the message boards where it began.

---

48   PJ Vogt and Alex Goldman, "Country of Liars," Gimlet Media, September 18, 2020.

The story takes viewers from the Philippines to South Africa. What they find is that QAnon is not a site helmed by an omnipotent government whistleblower as many followers believe. In fact, QAnon is a consortium of people. The likely primary culprit of the group who initiated many "Q drops," or beginning stories to inspire future conspiracies, is a South African programmer named Paul Furber.

QAnon followers believe they understand the real truth. The "Q drops" grow and are validated by members of the QAnon community. Followers find evidence to reveal the coded messages in the drops, trusting their like-minded peers to uncover a hidden reality. They know what is "really" happening behind the scenes of politics and society, and they believe the mainstream media would never cover the "real" truth. Vogt and Goldman uncover that conspiracy theorists (mostly white males) tend to trust their gut and increase their social media connections.

"The revolution in broadcast technology allows anyone to disseminate what he or she writes or says without intermediary and at no cost. This has displaced the gatekeepers, the producers, editors, and scholars who decided what was worthy of dissemination. The way is opened for conspiracy entrepreneurs who initiate and disseminate a seemingly infinite array of wild accusations," writes Muirhead and Rosenblum.

QAnon followers are far from the only group to create their own realities. Take for example the Proud Boys, the now banned alt-right movement, and, of course, the infamous neo-Nazi Richard Spencer.

Populist movements fueled by technology and online groups are a serious threat to liberal democracies around the world. Trump, a self-proclaimed populist, is proof that the power of digital technologies can be used to manipulate and mislead when in the hands of a nefarious storyteller.

The rise of new media has intrinsically led to the rise of populist-style movements in the United States. We consume more and more information in our digital bubbles, and that narrowness has led us to be more easily manipulated. We watch personal narrative stories that are designed to appeal to our emotions and confirm our worldview, and we believe them.

We don't want to interact with stories that contain opposing views because they make us feel uncomfortable and vulnerable. That lack of considering the other side has led to tremendous inward drilling in terms of our personal beliefs. By taking advantage of the digital boom and appealing to voters on a personal level, Trump drew a clear line in the United States—either you're with him or against him. He deepened that divide with every national debate and every ludicrous scandal. And in that divide, only one person won: Trump.

Connecting with an individual's human truth is a key storytelling strategy. Story arcs that are often used by brands are also used by populist-style politicians like Trump.

Now more than ever, we have to be more discerning consumers of content. We have to look beyond our own echo chambers and make ourselves vulnerable to contrary thoughts. It's up to the individual to question our emotional reactions and seek truth in what we read, watch, and listen to. If we're able to become more judicious, we may be able to support the storytelling that is based in reality: storytelling from the socially conscious storytellers. And if that spreads across society as quickly and decisively as conspiracy theories touted by Trump, we may experience healing in the United States sooner than we think.

CHAPTER 10

USER-GENERATED CONTENT AND THE BRILLIANCE OF *THE REAL HOUSEWIVES*

———

We just have to get comfortable with the fact that the unpolished, more authentic and raw stuff is the right way to go—because it costs less money to do it, you can turn it around faster, and people are going to want to engage with it more.

TIM LEAKE, CHIEF MARKETING AND
INNOVATION OFFICER, RPA ADVERTISING

The rise of new conspiracy theories isn't the only consequence of personal narrative storytelling. It's also made way for personal brand entrepreneurs, reality TV stars, and the phenomenon of influencers.

The media-tech sphere of today has made us all celebrities. Our online brand, how we are perceived by others in a digital space, is increasingly consequential to our lives. We star in our own Truman-esque TV shows online and show off the inner workings of our lives—the good, the bad, and the ugly.

Our social and digital channels have transformed not only the way we communicate but what we communicate about. Because of the accessibility and ease, we're more likely to share the mundane—a drive to school with the kids, a great sandwich we had on our lunch break, or a beautiful vista from an afternoon walk. The increased frequency with which we share the minutiae of our lives gives the impression we are ostensibly transparent. Of course, much has been written about the ways in which social media is a selective view into someone's life—a highlight reel of sorts as many people are reticent to share their darker or more difficult moments. Nonetheless, there are more opportunities now than ever to let the world in. The more personal our stories are, the more trust we tend to build with our family, friends, and followers.

In 2015, I was going through a rough breakup and decided to write about it:

"Whether you're the one to initiate the breakup or not, there is always a moment of regret. You're both still in love with one another, that's not the issue at hand. It's the involuntary circumstances, which are out of your control, that have put a strain on the bond: dependency issues, maintaining a sense of self, numerous insecurities, and unavoidable social pressures.

"Things that used to feel fake or at least controllable, have since transformed into a thick fog consuming your collective subconscious. Until finally, you can no longer see through the haze, and come to the heart-wrenching decision to break up."[49]

I write to process my feelings, and I had a lot of them during what was ultimately a mutually beneficial separation. But more interestingly, out of the hundreds of articles I've written, this garnered by far the most engagement.

When my family came across the article, they were shocked.

"How could you put this out into the world?" my mom asked.

I realized how desensitized I was to showing people my emotions. And I don't think I'm alone.

Entire generations (millennials and Gen Zers) are opening up online. Sharing personal anecdotes about yourself online is so commonplace, it's even come to be expected. It's not unusual for employers to review social channels during the job interview process and many online dating sites to link to your social media handles. These online spaces are often viewed as extensions of ourselves.

Reality TV has always been popular. But it's changed dramatically with the rise of UGC.

In *The Drama of Celebrity*, Marcus posits a new way of thinking about the media's relationship with celebrities that helps

---

49 Karam Sethi, "Four Phases of a Mutually Beneficial Break Up," The Huffington Post, September 14, 2015.

put celebrity culture in a theoretical framework for us to better understand the current moment.

"Celebrity culture is a drama involving three equally powerful groups: media producers, members of the public and celebrities themselves," she writes. "...all three compete and cooperate to assign value and meaning to celebrities...each of the three groups can create, spread, and interpret artful representations of famous people and their followers. Each requires the others in order to play, each can resist and undermine the others or collaborate with and cater to them; and each can, at least temporarily, influence, succumb to, or dominate the other two groups."[50]

Marcus uses numerous examples from history to illustrate her point. From Elvis Presley to Oscar Wilde, the relationship between the three groups requires *all* of us. Maybe none of her examples are more apt than Princess Diana. Diana was keenly aware of how to interact with the media, which is how, many argue, she became so beloved by the public.

"Diana knew how to work with the press to reach the public. Many plausibly considered her a savvy self-presenter who understood contemporary media relations far better than did other members of the royal family," Marcus writes. Though many in the family resented her for being so public, her consistent coverage captivated us, perched on the edge of our proverbial seats to see what she did next.

---

50 Sharon Marcus, The Drama of Celebrity, (New York: Princeton University Press, 2019) 230.

"Because publics, members of the media, and celebrities themselves all actively shape what it means to be a celebrity and to be interested in celebrities, their contests are too evenly matched for their outcomes to be easily predicted. That unpredictability makes celebrity culture a suspenseful, interactive, serial drama."

We love watching the real-life stories of celebrities unfold on social media, and unlike the 1990s and early 2000s when there were clear gatekeepers to celebrity stories (tabloids, *E!News*), we can now get stories straight from the source via platforms like Twitter and Instagram. "The most successful celebrities connect with fans in ways that bypass the media," Marcus notes.

As we've seen throughout this book, nefarious storytellers have just as much access as socially conscious storytellers do to the tools that can make themselves celebrities. As Diana was able to reach the public via media, so too has President Trump.

When analyzing Trump's relationship with and coverage by the media, Marcus notes the symbiotic relationship between the two.

"Faced with declining circulations, the press took advantage of Trump's savvy for galvanizing public attention. In advertising Trump, news outlets also advertised themselves," Marcus writes.

Not unlike Princess Diana, President Trump knew how to work with media outlets to reach the public (even if it was by villainizing them). When he wasn't able to reach his desired audience through traditional media, Trump was able to bypass them altogether and get his message across via his own social channels. Often, these tweets would in turn be covered by established media, garnering him coverage on the platform he initially sought.

The user-generated content on our feeds has no doubt enabled the rise of a new kind of celebrity. The phenomenon of UGC connects intimately with the reality TV genre, and the proliferation of self-infatuated storytellers. We love reality shows because they create seemingly authentic access and connection to the people at the center of the story.

As noted in the previous chapter, Marcus credits defiance as a way for celebrities to build an audience. Think about the Beatles proclaiming they were more popular than Jesus or Kim Kardashian famously breaking the internet when provocatively posing for the cover of *Paper* magazine in 2014. "Celebrities, by boldly making their shows of defiance public, do more than simply display unconventionality. They model an emotional attitude of indifference to nonconformity's potential consequences," Marcus writes.

Breaking social norms is commonplace across the reality TV genre.

There may be no better example of how defiance creates suspenseful drama than the *Real Housewives* franchise on the Bravo television network. These stars are apt examples of self-infatuated storytellers.

The media franchise started in 2006 in Orange County, California, with *The Real Housewives of Orange County*, a documentary-style look into the glamorous lifestyles of rich and famous OC residents.

According to a Bravo press release, the original idea of the show was inspired by scripted soap operas like *Peyton Place* and *Desperate Housewives*. People loved fictional rich people on TV. Why wouldn't they want to watch the real thing?[51]

In a recent interview, former *Real Housewives of New Jersey* cast member Caroline Manzo explains why people are infatuated with the show.

"I think that there are so many people out there that connect to every facet of our lives…If you don't connect with one you connect with another, there's something in all of us that everybody sees in their lives, good, bad, ugly, whatever."[52]

Despite the fact that these women have lifestyles the average viewer does not, the audience identifies with them, their relationships with one another, the businesses they run, and their struggles raising kids or navigating family dynamics. By allowing viewers into their lives, we feel as if they've entrusted us with something special. They trust us enough to showcase skeletons in their closets, so we trust them to be real and authentic.

---

51 Reality TV World Staff, "Bravo's 'The Real Housewives of Orange County' to premiere March 21," Reality TV World, January 6, 2006.

52 Chris Harnick, "What's the Secret to the Enduring Success of The Real Housewives?" EOnline, November 18, 2019.

Of course, some of it is scripted. Public wine fights may be coaxed by producers. But for the most part, it doesn't really matter if it's real or not. The connection we feel is real enough.

It would be reductive to say *The Real Housewives* is just about wealth and wine fights. The show tackles very real issues. Take for example Vicki Gunvalson's divorce with Donn Gunvalson in 2010. The two had been married for more than sixteen years, but their marriage had deteriorated over time.

"I want to be wanted. I want to be loved in my marriage," she says.[53] After many years, the two drifted apart and were seldom intimate.

That's something anyone who has been in a relationship can identify with. Just like the reason my written processing of my breakup connected with readers, watching Gunvalson process her own feelings connects with an emotional vulnerability we all possess.

While the franchises are often critiqued for racially homogenous and predominantly white casts, some *Real Housewives* stars talk about the experience of being nonwhite in America in the show. During the 2020 Black Lives Matters protests, Kandi Burruss (of *The Real Housewives of Atlanta*), Porsha Williams (of *The Real Housewives of Atlanta*), and Garcelle Beauvais (of *The Real Housewives of Beverly Hills*) came together for a Bravo special to discuss racial equality and justice in America. The series is called *Race in America: A Movement Not a Moment*.

---

53 The Real Housewives of Orange County, "Fashion Victim," Season 6, Episode 12, Bravo Network, May 22, 2011.

Williams, a star of the franchise, was arrested and tear-gassed twice while marching with United for Freedom organizers in protests over the deaths of Breonna Taylor and George Floyd. While proclaiming she is "a lot" on the show, she has used her platform to bring awareness to the important issues that affect her and many other people of color.

Reality television doesn't steer away from topics of nuance and politics. Rather, they make current events more accessible by relating them to the stars' personal lives.

The fights and petty drama draw us in: we don't tune in to Bravo to watch the news, after all. But to look past the increasingly complex subject matters these reality television series tackle —from family and health to politics and race—would be a disservice to Bravo producers and editors.

The authenticity in reality television is palpable on screen as well as off screen. The franchise has increasingly broken the fourth wall by allowing stars to decompress and elaborate about life issues covered on the show with fans on their Instagram handles and blogs.

They process arguments with costars. They have reunions of the season hosted by Andy Cohen. They do Facebook Lives. They even collaborate with social media influencers to create even more avenues to connect with fans. There is a whole marketing ecosystem built around the core twenty-episode season.

Eventually, the TV franchise just becomes a platform to build their brands. The actual *Real Housewives* franchise is inconsequential today. We care about Vicki Gunvalson, Luann de Lesseps, and Bethany Frankel, all no longer cast members on their respective shows. The franchise doesn't matter. UGC storytelling and new media have allowed these people to matter more than institutions. Bravo is simply one stage. There are many others. The self-infatuated storytellers of the show are stars and can go to their blogs, Twitter, Instagram, and Facebook to tell their stories.

And they do. The housewives are known for being digital entrepreneurs. They take to their social handles to sell perfume and handbag lines, but they also sell an ostensibly authentic line of communication to the storyteller.

UGC storytelling is a lucrative business. Beyond the checks the stars make from the Bravo network, they take their brands to an array of new business ventures.

Ashley and Michael Darby from *The Real Housewives of Potomac*, for example, launched a restaurant near Washington, DC. Oz was an Australian-themed restaurant where the Darbys were rarely seen. But regardless, fans went just to feel closer to the celebrities.

Kandi Burruss has an array of business ventures that include Bedroom Kandi, Kandi Koated Cosmetics, Old Lady Gang (a Southern eatery), Raising Ace, and Tags Boutique (luxury women's apparel). In addition to operating multiple companies, Burruss is a serial entrepreneur and has an extensive music portfolio, which includes a Grammy win and a Golden Note Award with her music group Xscape. Fans not only buy her products but flock to her speaking events and purchase her books.

The marketing ecosystem surrounding *The Real Housewives* franchise relies on the public's embrace of UGC.

Bravo made a successful gamble in the early 2000s and continues to double down. In 2019, they launched BravoCon, an event that brought together "bravolebrities" (what the network calls its reality TV stars) from across the network, from *The Real Housewives* to *Vanderpump Rules* and *Summer House.* Tickets to the three-day event in New York City went for up to $1,499.50. And they sold out.[54] The fame of the "Bravolebrities" grew through their UGC, and it clearly had lucrative outcomes.

Personal brands that rise to the top are those surrounded by drama, controversy, and fanfare. *The Apprentice*, perhaps Trump's most significant foray into mainstream media, is a great example of this.

The show began in 2004 as a reality game show. Contestants, unknown business people across industries, were broken up into teams to complete relatively ubiquitous business challenges, from selling products to executing advertising campaigns. Each episode ended with a signature moment: an elimination of one of the contestants by Trump yelling, "You're fired!" The grand prize at the end of each season was a one-year contract to work for Trump.

Trump, at the time, was in financial distress from his waning real-estate businesses and licensed his name not only

---

54   Lindsey Underwood, "14 Hours Inside the Church of BravoCon," The New York Times, November 19, 2019.

to make a consistent income but also to rebuild his image and increase the value of the Trump brand. The show, in many ways, created the Trump we know today. As James Poniewozik writes in the *New York Times*, Trump became "a Cap'n Crunch of capitalism, embodying a cartoon image of wealth and glamour."[55]

The Apprentice solidified Trump's media personality and brought leagues of new viewers to his doorstep—the perfect timing as platforms like Twitter and Facebook were on the rise in the early 2000s. Like the housewives, Trump could continue the show off air through his own user-generated stories.

Reality TV is rarely controversy-free.

The unfettered access that celebrities have to fans is neatly intertwined with the rise of UGC. It's led to more personal brands, entrepreneurs, and digital ventures. While an unlikely duo, *The Real Housewives* and FIPs have shown us what you can do with the power of digital storytelling. But they only represent part of the equation: self-infatuated storytellers and socially conscious storytellers, respectively. There are beneficiaries of the rise of UGC that have exploited digital tools to manipulate and dismantle reality.

"The revolution in broadcast technology that allows anyone to disseminate what he or she writes or says without intermediary and at no cost. This has displaced the gatekeepers, the producers, editors, and scholars who decided what was worthy of

---

55 James Poniewozik, "Donald Trump Was the Real Winner of 'The Apprentice,'" The New York Times, September 28, 2020.

dissemination. The way is opened for conspiracy entrepreneurs who initiate and disseminate a seemingly infinite array of wild accusations," writes Rosenblum and Muirhead.[56]

Categorizing groups who are taking advantage of the rise of UGC helps us think through how we want to use UGC storytelling in our lives.

Here is a recap of how I am defining these three groups:

The Nefarious Storyteller: Donald Trump represents the subset of people who use the digital revolution to lie, manipulate, and spread falsehoods to meet their own ends, like QAnon and 4chan. Trump was well equipped for a 2016 presidential run. He's been groomed by reality TV and was keenly aware UGC storytelling could sway the hearts and minds of voters. He fogged our minds while delegitimizing almost all types of mainstream news. Running the country was far different from running a business, but Trump knew politics could be twisted by entertaining UGC. If people liked watching feuds on *The Apprentice*, why wouldn't they like a conflict in a presidential campaign?

The Socially Conscious Storyteller: But there are also the historically disenfranchised who have been able to take advantage of the boom in technology to change their lives. Coss Marte, founder of CONBODY, didn't necessarily choose a personal branding path to create his fitness enterprise. He was subjugated to a fraught criminal justice system, then reentered

---

56   Russel Muirhead and Nancy L. Rosenblum, A Lot of People Are Saying, (New York: Princeton University Press, 2019) 58.

society without any job prospects open to him. He capitalized on the digital boom because he had no other options after his time in correctional facilities. But he was able to harness his narrative to propel his life forward. My father, an immigrant and someone who experiences racism regularly, also overcame many obstacles when he arrived in the United States. He was able to grow his brand and similarly harness his narrative to grow his dealership empire despite the obstacles put in front of him from society. Both men represent the best examples of the use of UGC. They have been able to benefit from the digital boom and find innovative ways of reaching audiences through social media.

The Self-Infatuated Storyteller: The stars of *The Real Housewives* and other reality TV represent the majority of UGC profiteers. They realize the benefits of the growing tide of personal stories but come from a clear place of privilege. They have many paths in front of them to choose from but see how they can reap the benefits of the current media technology ecosystem.

Why do we love reality TV personalities so much? Why does it feel like we love them more today than ever before?

Because we can see ourselves reflected in the emotional conflict we see in the lives of the celebrities.

Reality TV may be one of the most glaring examples of how the new media-tech sphere has driven a world run by UGC. But our obsessions with prying into the drama of a person's life isn't necessarily new. The talk show craze of the 1990s—*The Jerry Springer Show, Dr. Phil, The Maury Povich Show*—proves that.

Is this renewed focus on personal drama driven by the new, media-savvy self-infatuated storyteller's harmful society? It depends. Bombastic, physical, tabloid-style content will always have an audience. But the self-infatuated storyteller does not aim to lie or corrupt reality. I believe that is the critical difference between the nefarious storyteller and the self-infatuated storyteller. We will never stop being madly obsessed with drama. The danger lies in those who seek to use UGC and new media to break the ever-thinning divide between content and consumer with alluringly dramatic content aimed at distorting the consumers' reality.

CHAPTER 11

HOW USER-GENERATED CONTENT IS CHANGING THE WORLD

I believe at our best we can radically reconceptualize who we are…to the extent that we can accept our commonalities as human beings I think therein lies the key because then there is no one left to hate. That's not going to stop us from hating. But as Ernest Becker put it, maybe we can hate stuff that we should like poverty and injustice, and maybe we can then use righteous indignation to everybody's best interest.

DR. SHELDON SOLOMON, #UNFIT

It's hard to separate UGC from the detrimental impact it has had on society. Trump, QAnon, and other nefarious actors on the web are a creation of our own making.

We have a history of avidly consuming a particular sect of vulgar "info-tainment." Rupert Murdoch, CEO of multimedia conglomerate News Corp, was well aware of our obsession with tabloid-style content when he entered the media space. Murdoch ushered in a slew of ratings, grabbing shows like *America's Most Wanted* (1988), *COPS* (1989), and *When Animals Attack!* (1996), predecessors to the modern reality television genre. Tabloid-style-TV walked so *The Real Housewives* could run.

"If it bleeds, it leads," as the newsroom saying goes.

No doubt, we crave this kind of content. David Carr, venerated *New York Times* journalist, famously argued, "People tune in for the warfare. They're not interested in the fruits of peace. It's bad television. Who would want to watch that?"[57]

We can't look away from the drama-filled controversies, fights, yelling, war, or conspiracies. So what is the average consumer to do to reduce the grip nefarious storytellers have on us?

Nefarious storytellers prey on an attraction to tabloid drama. They spread falsehoods strategically veiled by compelling personal narratives. With every view, like, and share, we give their stories life, and that dissemination has a dangerous impact when it jumps off the screen and into real life.

There is no greater example of this than Trump's 2016 presidential campaign.

---

57 Reece Peck, Fox Populism, (New York: Cambridge University Press, 2019) 198.

George Conway, husband of Trump's White House counselor Kellyanne Conway, recently stated in the documentary *#Unfit*, "Donald Trump is like a practical joke that got out of hand."[58]

Trump is a controversial meme we thought funny enough to share because many never thought he'd win. His supporters saw the anger and resentment toward liberals that had been building for years reflected in his rhetoric, voting the "say it like it is" Republican candidate into office.

User-generated content is powerful. It can sway an election, spread religion, and create Fortune 500 businesses. From big tech to the White House, UGC touches all aspects of society today.

But I don't think that's the end of the story.

The boom in new media and accessibility to social platforms has also enabled people to use digital content to achieve more altruistic goals. Individuals like Coss Marte have been able to live more fruitful lives by building personal brands and crafting their own stories, via increasingly accessible storytelling platforms. Through digital tools the socially conscious storyteller has an opportunity to wrest back their own story. Historically disenfranchised members of society are able to share their stories, in their own voice, more broadly than ever before.

The past four years and 2020 in particular have been difficult for so many. A pandemic that swept the globe and a powerful

---

58 "#Unfit: The Psychology of Donald Trump," directed by Dan Partland (2020), Doc Shop Productions, on Amazon Prime.

racial justice movement in the United States have resulted in increased unrest, depression, and anxiety. But I don't believe these have won out in our collective psyche. Underneath the distress and despair there has been extraordinary hope—a hope for the future and a belief we can reshape our world into a better place for all. I believe altruism and good intent is still found in the digital creator community, but we are all too often distracted by the noise of drama and falsehoods to notice. Resigning ourselves to the inevitability of negative outcomes as a result of the digital boom is too easy. It doesn't account for the immensely positive change digital technologies have had on millions of people and the possibility that lies therein.

I believe empowering the socially conscious creator with better tools to tell their story can help increase the amount of purposeful and meaningful content on the internet. Increased dissemination of these stories can help us focus on issues that matter.

User-generated content is rapidly growing. Millennial consumers spend hours every day engaged with various types of media and 30 percent of that time is spent watching UGC. This is significant not only because of the sheer amount of time we spend watching UGC, but also the value we ascribe to it. Millennial consumers report UGC is 35 percent more memorable than other types of media.[59]

That means the photo posted by your best friend about her favorite coffee drink is significantly more memorable than the ad Starbucks made to promote it.

---

59 Jose Angelo Gallegos, "User-Generated Content Stats Study," Tint by Filestack, January 16, 2020.

Socially conscious storytellers are in a position to leverage influence for causes they care about and to campaign for the changes they want to see in society.

A character on the popular show *Insecure* serves as a fitting archetype for the socially conscious storyteller I'm describing.

Issa Dee, played by the cocreator of the show Issa Rae, lives in Los Angeles, California. She's twenty-nine years old and works as a youth liaison for the fictional nonprofit organization We Got Y'all. Dee is uncertain about her career but cares deeply about social justice and youth empowerment in marginalized communities, particularly in Los Angeles, the city in which she grew up. Most of the fourth season surrounds a block party–style event Dee organizes showcasing local artists and businesses. Rae, who also writes for the show, brings in real-life Los Angeles–based artists and businesses for the episode.[60]

Dee is passionate about her work and has a story to tell, but struggles to promote the event through word of mouth alone. She is (much to the audience's delight and relief) ultimately able to garner support from the community, book big-name headliners, and draw in huge crowds. But the question nagging at me was how much further she could have gone if she had access to better tools that could expand her reach and bring in an even larger audience.

There are countless Issa Dees in real life, trying to get their stories out in a crowded digital space. How much greater could their impact be if they had better tools to do so?

---

60   "Lowkey Moven' On," Insecure, Issa Rae, Season 4, Episode 5, HBO.

The COVID-19 pandemic and the 2020 Black Lives Matter protests have awakened new generations of digitally native activists.

In June 2020, six young girls came together to use their voices for positive change.

They, like so many, were shaken by the murders of Black men and women such as George Floyd and Breonna Taylor, feeling an urge to speak out in the face of injustice. Through their social media channels, they organized a protest to support racial justice in their hometown of Nashville, Tennessee, during their summer holiday.

Zee Thomas, Nya Collins, Emma Rose Smith, Mikayla Smith, Kennedy Green, and Jade Fuller all attended high school outside of Nashville.

"As teens, we feel like we cannot make a difference in this world, but we must," says Thomas in an interview with the *New York Times.*[61]

At fifteen years old, Thomas led a march of over ten thousand peaceful protesters through the streets of Nashville to call for racial justice in America.

Thomas and her friends have a story to tell. We must support these socially conscious storytellers not only through sharing their content but also by giving them the tools to increase their audience and tell their story in new ways.

---

61 Jessica Bennett, "These Teen Girls Are Fighting for a More Just Future," The New York Times, June 26, 2020.

In the near decade I've spent working in branding and advertising, and in the past four years specifically, I've seen the tremendous growth of brand partnerships with creators firsthand. Companies and brands understand the power of UGC and are endeavoring to harness it. By empowering digital content creators, we have established a booming new economic market: the creator economy. Now it's up to us to support socially conscious storytellers and make sure the rise in UGC is not overwhelmed by nefarious storytellers.

The digital boom has undoubtedly benefited tabloid news outlets like Fox News and populist political candidates like Trump who drive division and hate. But if we actively work to make sure socially conscious storytellers like Zee Thomas and Coss Marte get the tools they need to tell their stories to a digital audience better, we can start to shift the focus and drown out the noise.

In 2020, I launched Terra Digital to do just that.

If content is king, story is the castle. And the castle takes time, expertise, and budgets to build. We're on a mission to democratize video storytelling. Our software and tools automate templates (think explainers and how-tos) to provide a customizable starting point that shows users how to structure the beginning, middle, and end of a compelling narrative through video. We aim to empower those with a story to tell by giving them better tools with which to tell it.

By creating a platform for those who want to share their story in a compelling way but don't have large budgets to hire an agency or video editor, we make video creation attainable.

Think of Terra as a no-code website creation platform like Wix or Squarespace, but instead of web design, for video.

The proliferation of storytelling has created an opportunity we can't miss. We have the power to tell stories that matter, and the way we tell these stories to the world will define so much about our future.

There's an episode of *Bob's Burger*, an animated sitcom about a family running a hamburger restaurant, which illustrates my point.

Tina Belcher, eldest daughter of the Belcher family, auditions to be the anchor of Wagstaff School News, an all-student broadcast news show. After Tina auditions, faculty advisor Mr. Grant (voiced by Will Forte) argues the show must be controversial to bring in viewers. "Look, this news show competes for students' attention with cell phones, gossip, and bathroom graffiti. We need to be faster, meaner, and graffiti-er," he shouts.[62]

Tina, with no desire to sensationalize her story, breaks off to create her own broadcast. After watching both shows, the students laud Tina's straightforward, honest storytelling.

If we're able to empower the Tinas of the world with the right tools, we can sway the tech-media sphere back towards rationality and positivity.

---

62   "Broadcast Wagstaff School News," Bob's Burgers, Season 3, Episode 12, Fox.

This is a moment in which much about our shared experience is hard. But that difficulty has moved many to action. We want to do something. We want to use our voice. We want to act. Our own personal narratives have the power to make a positive impact by spreading awareness, educating, and advocating against injustice. It's easy to feel disheartened by the far-reaching influence and manipulation of nefarious storytellers. But I argue it is a blessing to gain that sort of awareness. Because now we can act on it.

Now is the time for change, and I, for one, am excited about it.

APPENDIX

INTRODUCTION: ANTHONY BOURDAIN'S UNLIKELY IMPACT ON THE WORLD OF STORY

Ghattas, Kim. "How Lebanon Transformed Anthony Bourdain." The Atlantic, June 2018.

"Myanmar." Part's Unknown. Directed by Anthony Bourdain. April 2013.

CHAPTER 1: STORYTELLING THROUGH THE AGES

"Railsplitter." House Divided. Published September 24, 2010. http://housedivided.dickinson.edu/sites/journal/2010/08/26/railsplitter/.

Leveen, Adriane. "Storytelling in the Bible." Society of Biblical Literature. Accessed January 12, 2021. https://www.sbl-site.org/assets/pdfs/TB4_Storytelling_AL.pdf.

Statista Research Department. "Leading cable TV series in the United States in Fall 2016, by number of viewers." Statista Database. Published September 19, 2016. https://www-statista-com.ezproxy.cul.columbia.edu/statistics/530240/series-viewers-usa/.

Tullai, Martin. "Abe Lincoln, Rail Splitter." The Baltimore Sun, February 13, 1995. https://www.baltimoresun.com/news/bs-xpm-1995-02-13-1995044042-story.html.

White, Michael. "Importance of the Oral Tradition." PBS. Published April 1998. https://www.pbs.org/wgbh/pages/frontline/shows/religion/story/oral.html.

CHAPTER 2: PRINCIPLES OF AUTHENTIC STORYTELLING

Cortada, James W. IBM: The Ride and Fall and Reinvention of a Global Icon. Hardback Edition. Cambridge, MA: MIT Press, 2019.

Robertson, Eric. "Monroe's Motivated Sequence | COMMUNICATION STUDIES." May 10, 2019. 16:23 minutes. https://www.youtube.com/watch?v=NdrJX5b4R-0.

Fusco, Jon. "The 6 Emotional Arcs of Storytelling, Why You Should Use Them, and Which One is Best," No Film School (blog), November 29, 2016, https://nofilmschool.com/2016/11/emotional-arcs-6-storytelling-kurt-vonnegut.

Godin, Seth. "Ode: How to tell a great story," Seth Godin (blog), April 27, 2006, https://seths.blog/2006/04/ode_how_to_tell/.

"Writing 101: What Is the Hero's Journey? 2 Hero's Journey Examples in Film," Masterclass (blog), Oct 2, 2020, https://www.masterclass.com/articles/writing-101-what-is-the-heros-journey#joseph-campbell-and-the-heros-journey.

Peck, Reece. Fox Populism. New York: Cambridge University Press, 2019.

Staff, "Good Design Is Good Business," IBM Icons in Progress Blog.

Stoll, Julia. "Reasons for watching reality TV in the United States as of March 2017, by age." Statista Database, published on Jan 27, 2021. https://www.statista.com/statistics/692685/reasons-watching-reality-tv-age/.

Syckle, Katie Van. "Why The Times Crowdsources Reporting." The New York Times, July 19, 2018. https://www.nytimes.com/2018/07/19/insider/user-generated-content-ugc.html#:~:text=Photos%2C%20videos%20and%20digitally%20submitted,citizen%2C%20captured%20President%20John%20F.

Quito, Anne. "IBM has freed itself from the tyranny of Helvetica." Quartz, November 10, 2017. https://qz.com/1124664/ibm-plex-with-its-first-ever-custom-corporate-font-ibm-is-freeing-itself-from-the-tyranny-of-helvetica/.

CHAPTER 4: MY JOURNEY INTO STORYTELLING
Bauerlein, Valerie. "Lessons Learned from the Response to Katrina's Havoc." Wall Street Journal, August 28, 2015. https://www.wsj.com/articles/lessons-learned-from-failed-response-to-katrina-1440787007.

Sethi, Karam. "Emotional Intelligence and Empathy for Effective Leadership with Thad Allen." Booz Allen Big Ideas Podcast. October 11, 2015. https://soundcloud.com/boozallen/sets/booz-allen-big-ideas-presented.

CHAPTER 5: AUTHENTIC STORYTELLING AND THE FALL OF THE BRAND
Heusner, Michael. "Millennials want brands to communicate more during COVID-19 crisis, study finds." Campaign, April 1, 2020. https://www.campaignlive.com/article/millennials-want-brands-communicate-during-covid-19-crisis-study-finds/1678922.

Customer Guru. Net promoter Score. McDonalds. https://customer.guru/net-promoter-score/mcdonald-s.

Ethan, Cramer-Flood. "US Average Time Spent per Day with Digital Video." eMarketer. February 4, 2020. https://content-na1.emarketer.com/us-time-spent-with-media-2021-update.

Haddon, Heather. "McDonald's Sales Fall as Coronavirus Pandemic Changes Dining Habits." Wall Street Journal, April 3, 2020. https://www.wsj.com/articles/mcdonalds-sales-drop-6-11588248343#:~:text=MCD%20%2D1.68%25%20said%20dramatic%20changes,expects%20to%20continue%20for%20months.&text=Chief%20Executive%20Chris%20Kempczinski%20said,look%20like%20in%20the%20future.

Isaac, Mike. "Uber Founder Travis Kalanick Resigns as C.E.O." The New York Times, September 19, 2017.

McNamee, Roger. "A Primer to Big Tech's Antitrust Hearing: They're (Almost) All Guilty." Wired, July 24, 2020.

Staff. "LGBTQ Pride Consumerism." Wired, June 21, 2018.

Yadav, Yash. "Full Pepsi Commercial Starring Kendal Jenner." April 6, 2017. 2:48 minutes. https://www.youtube.com/watch?v=uwvAgDCOdU4.

CHAPTER 6: RISE OF PERSONAL NARRATIVE CONTENT

"#Unfit: The Psychology of Donald Trump." Directed by Dan Partland (2020). Doc Shop Productions. On Amazon Prime.

Chaney, Jen. "Andrew Cuomo's Daily Press Briefing Is the Most Important Show on TV." Vulture, March 26, 2020. https://www.vulture.com/2020/03/andrew-cuomos-press-briefing-is-great-tv.html.

Gstalter, Morgan. "Cuomo brothers rib each other during CNN interview: 'There's always a time to call mom.'" The Hill, March 17, 2020. https://thehill.com/homenews/media/488025-cuomo-brothers-rib-each-other-during-cnn-interview-theres-always-a-time-to.

Mehta, Dhrumil. "Most Americans Like How Their Governor Is Handling The Coronavirus Outbreak." FiveThirtyEight. April 20, 2020. https://fivethirtyeight.com/features/most-americans-like-how-their-governor-is-handling-the-coronavirus-outbreak/.

Reilly, Katie. "Read Hillary Clinton's 'Basket of Deplorables' Remarks About Donald Trump Supporters." Time, September 10, 2016.

CHAPTER 7: USER-GENERATED CONTENT & THE CITIZEN

Peck, Reece. Fox Populism. New York: Cambridge University Press, 2019.

Schudson, Michael. The Good Citizen. Reprint Edition. New York: Free Press, 2011.

Schudson, Michael. "The Good Citizen." C-Span. 1998. https://www.c-span.org/video/?114821-1/the-good-citizen/.

CHAPTER 8: EMPOWERING THE SOCIALLY CONSCIOUS STORYTELLER

Bodarky, George. "From Jail Cell To Studio: Drug Dealer Becomes Personal Trainer." National Public Radio. January 2, 2015. https://www.npr.org/2015/01/02/371894920/from-jail-cell-to-studio-drug-dealer-becomes-personal-trainer.

Gross, Courtney. "NEW YORK'S PRISON PIPELINE." Metrofocus/NY1. March 15, 2018.
https://www.thirteen.org/metrofocus/2018/03/new-yorks-prison-pipeline/.

Saffo, Paul. "Paul Saffo: The Creator Economy." The Long Now. March 31, 2015.
https://longnow.org/seminars/02015/mar/31/creator-economy/.

Selby, Daniele. "The Surprising Mission Behind Conbody'S 'Prison-Style'
Workouts." Global Citizen. May 15, 2019.
https://www.globalcitizen.org/en/content/conbody-coss-marte-former-prisoner-fitness/.

Staff. "Support Grows For Restoration Of Voting Rights To Formerly Incarcerated
People In Alabama." Equal Justice Initiative. February 1, 2016.
https://eji.org/news/growing-support-restore-voting-rights-formerly-
incarcerated-alabamians/.

Stevenson, Bryan. Just Mercy. Trade Paperback Edition. New York: Random House, 2015.

Vee, Gary. "CONBODY's Coss Marte chats with #GaryVee on
#MarketingForTheNow episode #8!" YouTube Video. 16:01. August 3, 2020.
https://www.youtube.com/watch?v=sBscXvPuFuE.

CHAPTER 9: PERSONAL NARRATIVE STORYTELLING, CONSPIRACY THEORIES, AND THE DARK SIDE OF THE DIGITAL BOOM

Dropp, Kyle and Nyhan, Brendan. "It Lives. Birtherism Is Diminished but Far From
Dead." The New York Times, September 23, 2016.

Marcus, Sharon. The Drama of Celebrity. Princeton University Press. 2019.

Muirhead, Russel and Rosenblum, Nancy L. A Lot of People Are Saying. Princeton
University Press. Preface to paperback edition: Princeton, New Jersey. 2019

Muller, Jan-Werner. What is Populism? University of Pennsylvania Press. 2016.

Sebastion, Michael and Bruney, Gabrielle. "What is Pizzagate?" Esquire, July 24, 2020.
https://www.esquire.com/news-politics/news/a51268/what-is-pizzagate/.

Ransom, Jan. "Trump Will Not Apologize for Calling for Death Penalty Over
Central Park Five." The New York Times, June 18, 2019.
https://www.nytimes.com/2019/06/18/nyregion/central-park-five-trump.html.

Vogt, PJ and Goldman, Alex. "Country of Liars." Gimlet Media. September 18, 2020.
https://gimletmedia.com/shows/reply-all/llhe5nm.

CHAPTER 10: USER-GENERATED CONTENT AND THE BRILLIANCE OF THE REAL HOUSEWIVES

Harnick, Chris. "What's the Secret to the Enduring Success of The Real
Housewives?" EOnline. November 18, 2019.
https://www.eonline.com/news/1094540/what-s-the-secret-to-the-enduring-
success-of-the-real-housewives.

Marcus, Sharon. The Drama of Celebrity. New York: Princeton University Press. 2019.

Muirhead, Russel and Rosenblum, Nancy L. A Lot of People Are Saying. Princeton University Press. Preface to paperback edition: Princeton, New Jersey. 2019.

Poniewozik, James. "Donald Trump Was the Real Winner of 'The Apprentice.'" The New York Times, September 28, 2020.
https://www.nytimes.com/2020/09/28/arts/television/trump-taxes-apprentice.html.

Reality TV World Staff. "Bravo's 'The Real Housewives of Orange County' to premiere March 21." Reality TV World. January 6, 2006.
https://www.realitytvworld.com/news/bravo-the-real-housewives-of-orange-county-premiere-march-21-3897.php.

Sethi, Karam. "Four Phases of a Mutually Beneficial Break Up." The Huffington Post, September 14, 2015.
https://www.huffpost.com/entry/four-phases-of-a-mutually_b_8136958.

The Real Housewives of Orange County. "Fashion Victim." Season 6. Episode 12. Bravo Network.

Underwood, Lindsey. "14 Hours Inside the Church of BravoCon." The New York Times, November 19, 2019.
https://www.nytimes.com/2019/11/19/style/bravocon-2019.html.

CHAPTER 11: HOW USER-GENERATED CONTENT IS CHANGING THE WORLD

"#Unfit: The Psychology of Donald Trump." Directed by Dan Partland (2020). Doc Shop Productions. On Amazon Prime.

Bennett, Jessica. "These Teen Girls Are Fighting for a More Just Future." The New York Times, June 26, 2020.
https://www.nytimes.com/2020/06/26/style/teen-girls-black-lives-matter-activism.html.

"Broadcast Wagstaff School News." Bob's Burgers. Season 3. Episode 12. Fox.

Gallegos, Jose Angelo. "User-Generated Content Stats Study." Tint by Filestack. January 16, 2020.
https://www.tintup.com/blog/user-generated-content-stats-study/

Peck, Reece. Fox Populism. New York: Cambridge University Press, 2019.

"Lowkey Moven' On." Insecure. Issa Rae. Season 4. Episode 5. HBO.

ACKNOWLEDGMENTS

Eliza McNabb

Latika Sethi

Simran Sodhi

Mehar Sethi

Mamie Gummer

Peter Sethi

Vaas Sethi

Dalip Singh Sethi